The politics of exclusion

Published in our
centenary year
～ **2004** ～
MANCHESTER
UNIVERSITY
PRESS

ISSUES IN GERMAN POLITICS
Edited by
Professor Charlie Jeffery, Institute for German Studies
Dr Charles Lees, University of Sheffield

Issues in German Politics is a major new series on contemporary Germany. Focusing on the post-unity era, it presents concise, scholarly analyses of the forces driving change in domestic politics and foreign policy. Key themes will be the continuing legacies of German unification and controversies surrounding Germany's role and power in Europe. The series includes contributions from political science, international relations and political economy.

Already published:

Annesley: *Postindustrial Germany: Services, technological transformation and knowledge in unified Germany*

Bulmer, Jeffery and Paterson: *Germany's European diplomacy: Shaping the regional milieu*

Gunlicks: *The* Länder *and German federalism*

Harding and Paterson (eds): *The future of the German economy: An end to the miracle?*

Harnisch and Maull (eds): *Germany as a Civilian Power? The foreign policy of the Berlin Republic*

Hyde-Price: *Germany and European order: Enlarging NATO and the EU*

Lees: *The Red–Green coalition in Germany: Politics, personalities and power*

Rittberger (ed.): *German foreign policy since unification: Theories and case studies*

The politics of exclusion

Institutions and immigration policy in contemporary Germany

Simon Green

Manchester University Press

Manchester and New York

Distributed exclusively in the USA by Palgrave

Published by Manchester University Press
Oxford Road, Manchester M13 9NR, UK
and Room 400, 175 Fifth Avenue, New York, NY 10010, USA
www.manchesteruniversitypress.co.uk

Distributed exclusively in the USA by
Palgrave, 175 Fifth Avenue, New York,
NY 10010, USA

Distributed exclusively in Canada by
UBC Press, University of British Columbia, 2029 West Mall,
Vancouver, BC, Canada V6T 1Z2

British Library Cataloguing-in-Publication Data
A catalogue record for this book is available from the British Library

Library of Congress Cataloging-in-Publication Data applied for

ISBN   0 7190 6588 7 *hardback*

First published 2004

13 12 11 10 09 08 07 06 05 04   10 9 8 7 6 5 4 3 2 1

Typeset in Minion by Carnegie Publishing Ltd, Lancaster
Printed in Great Britain by Biddles Ltd, King's Lynn

For my parents

Contents

Tables

Acknowledgements

This monograph would not be complete without mention of the range of friends, colleagues and family to whom I owe both an intellectual and personal debt of gratitude. First and foremost among these are William Paterson and Charlie Jeffery at the Institute for German Studies. Both have been mentors in the truest sense of the word, and I am deeply grateful for their unstinting support. During my first research stay in Germany in 1996, which was generously funded by the Deutscher Akademischer Austauschdienst (DAAD), I was very fortunate to have been supported by a large number of people. I am especially indebted to Thomas Kossendey MdB, who gave me the opportunity to pursue my research from within the *Bundestag*. Later that year, Dietrich Thränhardt at the University of Münster kindly provided me with a base from which I could conduct further research as well as a sounding board for some initial conclusions. I am also extremely grateful to my interview partners over the years, most of whom preferred to remain anonymous. All were, without exception, generous with their time and extremely open to my questions. Their experiences and judgements provided me with invaluable background information and insights into this policy area.

In addition, many colleagues and friends have at various stages over the past years contributed to the intellectual fermentation process that is academic research. These have included Gisbert Brinkmann, Sebastian Edathy MdB, Jonathan Grix, Jürgen Haberland, Heike Hagedorn, Dan Hough, Jeremy Jennings, Barbara John, Zig Layton-Henry, Charles Lees, Kerry Longhurst, Paul McVeigh, Hans-Heinrich Nolte and Patrick Weil. In particular, I would especially like to thank Randall Hansen, who over many years has shown a tireless willingness to debate the finer points of German nationality policy with me. This is undoubtedly a rare quality.

On a personal level, my wife, Insa Nolte, deserves particular recognition and thanks for providing unfailing support, encouragement and suggestions over the years, as well as indispensable proofreading and checking services. I am deeply indebted to her for this. Finally, I would like to thank my parents, Tina and Bryan Green, who, more than fifteen years ago, first introduced me to the issues covered here. In every respect, I owe them a lot, and it is therefore to them that I dedicate this book.

Simon Green
Birmingham

Glossary of terms

Anwerbestopp	Ban on further recruitment of guestworkers of 23 November 1973
Asyl	Political asylum
Asylbewerber	Asylum seekers
Asylverfahrengesetz	lit. 'Asylum Procedural Law'
Ausländer	Non-national (foreign) resident of Germany
Ausländeraufnahmegesetz	lit. 'Foreigners' Entry Law'
Ausländergesetz	lit. 'Foreigners' Law', passed in 1965 and revised in 1990
Ausländerintegrationsgesetz	lit. 'Foreigners' Integration Law'
Ausländerpolizeiverordnung	lit. 'Foreigners' Police Decree'
Aussiedler	Ethnic German immigrants (from 1950 to 1992)
Aussiedleraufnahmegesetz	lit. 'Ethnic German Entry Law'
Duldung	Temporary but renewable stay of deportation, usually on humanitarian or practical grounds
Ehegattenachzug	Dependant migration of spouses
Einbürgerungszusicherung	lit. 'naturalisation guarantee'
Einwanderung/Zuwanderung	Immigration
Familiennachzug	Family reunification or dependant migration
Fraktion	Parliamentary party
Gastarbeiter	lit. 'guestworkers'
Grundgesetz	Basic Law (constitution) of Germany
Ius domicili	Citizenship based on residence

Ius sanguinis	Principle of descent for ascription of citizenship at birth
Ius soli	Territorial principle of ascription of citizenship at birth
Kindernachzug	Dependant migration of minors
Kinderstaatszugehörigkeit/ Kinderstaatsangehörigkeit	Special citizenship provisions for children born in Germany to non-national parents
Kriegsfolgenbereinigungs-gesetz	lit. 'Law for the Resolution of Consequences Arising from the War'
Optionsmodell	Policy by which children with dual nationality must, under certain circumstances, choose between their German and other nationality by the age of twenty-three
Rechtsanspruch (pl. Rechtsansprüche)	Legal entitlement to policy provision
Regelanspruch	Entitlement 'as a rule' to policy provision
Reichs- und Staatsangehörigkeitsgesetz (RuStAG)	Citizenship Law of 1913, revised in 1999
Spätaussiedler	Ethnic German immigrants (after 1 January 1993)
Staatsangehörigkeit	Citizenship
Übersiedler	GDR refugees
Vetriebene	German war refugees, 1945–49
Zuwanderer	Immigrants
Zuwanderungsgesetz	Immigration Law

Note on terminology and sources

In the interests of accessibility, all German-language quotes throughout the book have been translated into English. Accordingly, the book will normally refer to 'foreigners' or 'non-nationals' as the direct translation of the formally correct German term *Ausländer*, and only use the more common English term 'immigrants' where specifically appropriate. However, the ambiguities over the terms' English usage are acknowledged. All ministers and ministries are at federal level unless otherwise stated. *Ausländergesetz* will refer to the 1990 version, while the original 1965 law will be designated by that year. 'Germany' will generally refer to West Germany before 1990 and united Germany from then on. The term 'European Union' (EU) will be the sole term used to refer to the institutions of European integration since 1957.

Unless otherwise stated, all statistical data cited in this book is taken from the following sources: the Federal Statistical Office (Statistisches Bundesamt, via: www.destatis.de), the Federal Office for the Recognition of Foreign Refugees (Bundesamt für die Anerkennung ausländischer Flüchtlinge, via: www.bafl.de) and reports published by the Federal Commissioner for Foreigners' Affairs (Beauftragte der Bundesregierung für Ausländerfragen, via: www.integrationsbeauftragte.de).

1
Understanding *Ausländerpolitik* in Germany

Everyone who is not German in the sense of Article 116 Paragraph 1 of the
Basic Law is a foreigner. (Section 1 *Ausländergesetz*)

What at first sight seems nothing more than an innocuous, almost
self-evident provision of a piece of legislation is in fact the gateway to
a policy minefield. For behind its seductive simplicity, which has constituted a mainstay of German policy towards immigrants and
non-national residents for over thirty-five years, lies a web of complex
legal provisions, which affects and regulates the lives of almost every
tenth inhabitant of Germany. Since the mid-1950s, *Ausländerpolitik*, as
this policy area is known in German, has been and remains one of the
central issues of the German domestic political agenda.

The definition of *Ausländerpolitik* is not as easy as might at first be
expected. The term is a deceptively simple one to cover an enormous
range of issues and is very difficult to conceive of in English. Translated literally as 'policy towards foreigners', none of the terms
'immigration policy', 'residence policy', 'integration policy' or 'citizenship policy' alone adequately captures its meaning; instead, it covers
all of these together. Table 1.1 provides a summary of the different
principal dimensions of *Ausländerpolitik* and their various legal bases in
2002.

In fact, the precise definition of *Ausländerpolitik* is still more complex.
As the right-hand column in Table 1.1 shows, not all immigrants are
technically foreign: ethnic Germans have constituted one of the main
sources of immigration to Germany. At the same time, not all foreigners
are immigrants: Germany's exclusive reliance on the principle of descent
(*ius sanguinis*) in the ascription of its citizenship at birth before 2000
has meant that second- and third-generation immigrants have grown
up in Germany without automatic access to nationality. Inevitably, this
creates difficulties over the accurate use of labels, especially in English
(cf. Faist, 1994): in contrast to the UK, immigrants and non-nationals

Table 1.1 Principal dimensions and legal bases of immigration, residence and citizenship policy in Germany, 2002

Immigrants [a]	Asylum seekers (*Asylbewerber*)	Family reunification (*Familiennachzug*)	War refugees (*Bürgerkriegs flüchtlinge*)	Ethnic Germans (*Spätaussiedler*)
... are defined by ...	*Asylpolitik*	*Ausländerpolitik*	*Flüchtlingspolitik*	*Aussiedlerpolitik*
	↓	↓	↓	↓
... and are allowed to enter the FRG in accordance with:	Article 16a GG, Geneva Convention AsylVfG	Sections 17–23, 31 AuslG	Section 32a AuslG	Article 116 [1] GG, BVFG, KfBG, AAG, WoZuG
	↓	↓	↓	↓
Once in Germany,[b] residence is codified in ...		*Ausländerpolitik*		↓
	↓	↓	↓	↓
... which has the following legal basis:	Sections 24–7, 51–7 AuslG, AsylBewLG	Sections 15–16, 24–7 AuslG	Sections 35, 51–7 AuslG	↓
	↓	↓	↓	↓
The acquisition of citizenship is covered by ...		*Ausländerpolitik/Staatsangehörigkeitsrecht*		*Staatsangehörig-keitsrecht*
		↓		↓
... and is granted under conditions laid down in the following legislation:		Sections 85–9 AuslG; Sections 8–9 StAG; EinbRili		Article 116 [1] GG, StAngRegG (NB granted before arrival in Germany)

Notes:
[a] In 2002, no permanent immigration by any other groups of people (such as labour migrants) was permitted, except by temporary labour migration for seasonal purposes, as well as by high-skilled workers in the IT sector (the so-called 'Green Card' programme). In addition, EU citizens are exempted from all immigration law, but a simplified residential framework still applies to them.
[b] Includes children of non-national parents born in Germany.
AAG = Aussiedleraufnahmegesetz; AsylBewLG = Asylbewerberleistungsgesetz; AsylVfG = Asylverfahrensgesetz; AuslG = Ausländergesetz; BVFG = Bundesvertriebenen- und Flüchtlingsgesetz; EinbRili = Einbürgerungsrichtlinien; FRG = Federal Republic of Germany; GG = Grundgesetz; KfBG = Kriegsfolgenbereinigungsgesetz; StAG = Staatsangehörigkeitsgesetz; StAngRegG = Gesetz zur Regelung von Fragen der Staatsangehörigkeit; WoZuG = Wohnortzuweisungsgesetz.

in Germany tend to be classified by nationality and not country of birth or ethnic origin.

The subject of this book, then, is an analysis of Germany's post-war *Ausländerpolitik*, especially between 1955 and 2002, undertaken from the perspective of policy-making. However, while most of the dimensions in Table 1.1 will be addressed at various points of this analysis, it would be impossible to cover all aspects exhaustively; in particular, asylum and ethnic German migration are already the subject of quite an extensive sub-field of scholarship (e.g. Münch, 1992; Angenendt, 1997; Marshall, 2000; see also Rock and Wolff, 2002). Instead, the primary focus here will be on three aspects of *Ausländerpolitik*: immigration, principally in the form of secondary or dependant migration; policy towards foreigners with ordinary residence (i.e. excluding asylum seekers); and citizenship policy, in terms of the conditions both for ascription at birth and naturalisation in later (often adult) life.

But why devote an entire book towards such a specific policy area, and why now? For the first question, two main reasons may be identified. First, immigration and asylum (*Ausländer/Asyl*) have concerned the German public to a greater or lesser extent for more than twenty years, as the Forschungsgruppe Wahlen's monthly and highly respected *Politbarometer* surveys of public opinion have shown: ever since 1980, the two issues together have repeatedly been judged to be one of Germany's most pressing political problems (Forschungsgruppe Wahlen, 2000). From September 1991 to summer 1993, the percentage of respondents for whom the issue was the most important at times exceeded 60 per cent, a record at that time. Only following the amendment in 1993 of the asylum provision in Article 16 of Germany's constitution, the Basic Law (*Grundgesetz*), did the issue begin to lose in importance. However, despite gradually dropping off, the *Ausländer* issue remained in the top three issues until January 1997, and briefly returned there in early 1999, during the controversy over the formulation of the current citizenship law. Even though its current resonance among the population is lower, its values in 1992 and 1993 show the potential this issue has.

Second, immigration can, on occasions, also be very important electorally. Chapters 3 and 4 will illustrate the impact of extreme right-wing parties on politics in the 1980s and early 1990s. More recently, the extremist German People's Union (*Deutsche Volksunion*, DVU), campaigning on an overt anti-foreigner platform, scored almost 13 per cent of the vote in the Saxony-Anhalt state (*Land*, plural *Länder*) election of

26 April 1998, the best ever for such a party in the history of the Federal
Republic. In its aftermath, conservative parties reacted by re-emphasising their own commitment to a tough line on *Ausländerpolitik*
(*Guardian*, 28 April 1998). This tactic was repeated in the run-up to
the 2002 federal election, when the conservative chancellor candidate
(*Kanzlerkandidat*), the Bavarian Minister-President Edmund Stoiber,
explicitly played up fears of immigrant extremists in the hope of
making an impact during the dying days of the campaign (*Guardian*,
19 September 2002). As the *Wall Street Journal Europe* soberly noted
on 23 September 1998, shortly before that year's federal election, 'the
immigration issue holds political dynamite in Germany'.

As well as immigration, residence and citizenship policy standing out
for their importance in German politics as a whole, the policy sector
per se is quite unlike any other in the domestic politics of industrialised
countries. For all other policy areas deal primarily with nationals of the
country concerned, in that they define, regulate or formalise the relationship between the state and its citizens. By contrast, *Ausländerpolitik*
is the only domestic German policy sector to deal exclusively with
non-citizens, who in theory have no political control mechanism, in the
form of voting rights, available to them.

The answer to why this study is timely now, at the beginning of a
new millennium, lies in the nature and effects of immigration to
Germany. In themselves, these require some explanation. Over the past
fifty years, West Germany (and united Germany since 1990) has been
the destination of almost 30 million immigrants, the vast majority of
whom have settled permanently (Münz and Ulrich, 1999; see also full
breakdown of migration flows in Beauftragte der Bundesregierung,
2001). Around 15 million persons, or half of this total, have been of
German origin:

• Around 8 million refugees arrived in West Germany in the
  immediate post-war years

• 3 million East Germans (*Übersiedler*) fled the GDR in the period
  up to the construction of the wall in 1961

• Just over 4 million ethnic Germans (*Aussiedler*, from 1993
  Spätaussiedler) migrated to Germany from Poland, Romania or
  the former Soviet Union between 1950 and 2001, of which
  around 40 per cent arrived in the last fourteen years of that
  period.

However, the remainder has been of non-ethnic German origin, and therefore of non-German nationality. During the 1960s and 1970s, immigration was largely in the form of labour migrants, which West Germany, along with many other western European countries, recruited in the pre-oil shock boom years. Although the majority of this migration was only temporary, some 3 million non-nationals remained in the country when recruitment ended in 1973 and were soon joined by spouses and dependants. While German statistics do not differentiate by purpose of entry (i.e. whether labour migrants or their dependants), these two groups together constitute the rump of Germany's non-national community. Indeed, dependant migration from outside the European Union (EU) remains a major source of immigration to this day (cf. Appendix, p. 144).

From the late 1970s onwards, asylum became an important entry route to Germany. With its strong economy, large established migrant communities and a unique constitutional guarantee of political asylum, Germany received over 2.8 million applications for asylum between 1977 and 2002; around 43 per cent of these were lodged in the space of just four years between 1990 and 1993. The vast majority of applications were rejected (over 90 per cent between 1985 and 2001), due principally to Germany's narrow interpretation of the grounds for asylum to exclude non-state agents of persecution (e.g. local militia) and gender-specific oppression (e.g. genital mutilation). Nonetheless, many failed asylum seekers have been able to remain in the country, often for humanitarian reasons.[1] Finally, the 1990s saw the arrival of around 350,000 temporary war refugees from Bosnia-Herzegovina and Kosovo. By the end of 2002, over 7.3 million non-nationals were resident in Germany, a figure which itself has increased by over one-third, or almost 2 million persons, since unification in 1990 (see Appendix). On 31 December 2002, foreigners accounted for 8.9 per cent of the population, one of the highest levels in the EU, and included almost 2 million Turkish nationals, 1.9 million EU nationals and 1 million citizens of the former Yugoslavia. In total, there were twenty nationalities with at least 50,000 persons resident in Germany. This spread, when combined with the various types of immigration that have taken place, has meant that Germany's foreign population is both large and highly diverse. For a country without a long colonial history, and one which, during the nineteenth century, was characterised by emigration rather than immigration, this influx has posed a considerable social and political challenge.

The nature of this challenge is highlighted by one of the most notorious paradoxes of modern politics: despite substantial immigration over a period of several decades, government policy steadfastly maintained that Germany was 'not a country of immigration' (*Deutschland ist kein Einwanderungsland*). The almost dogmatic resolve with which successive governments until 1998 pushed this line stands in stark contrast to the statistical reality: at the end of 2002, the average residence period of the 7.3 million foreigners in Germany was 15.3 years; two-thirds had lived in Germany for eight or more years, and one-third for more than twenty years. Yet if anything, such figures actually underestimate the true degree of settlement among many non-nationals in Germany. On the one hand, the proportion of non-nationals with over twenty years' residence rises sharply among those nationalities from whom labour was recruited in the 1960s and 1970s, such as Turkey. On the other hand, the figures do not reflect the fact that those foreign residents who were born in Germany (some 1.6 million persons or 21 per cent of the total in 2002) have lived in the country all their lives. Thus a four year-old non-national child born in Germany is statistically counted as having just four years' residence, despite these four years covering its entire life. It was developments such as these which prompted Dietrich Thränhardt to famously describe Germany as an 'undeclared country of immigration' (Thränhardt, 1988).

As this book will go on to illustrate, the denial of being a country of immigration has permeated government policy over several decades. Justified by the fact that Germany was not seeking new permanent immigration, governments did not bother to put into place many of the formal policy structures which are common in other countries where immigration has been more readily acknowledged; on the contrary, for many years residence and citizenship policies were defined on an exclusionary basis, rather than on the inclusionary basis the sheer quantity of immigration to Germany would otherwise have merited (Green, 2003). The fact that non-ethnic German immigration continued in the form of dependant migration (otherwise known as family reunification) and asylum seekers throughout the 1980s and 1990s meant that the 'non-immigration' policy came to be heavily contested both between and within political parties.

The sometimes surreal political debate over whether or not Germany was actually a country of immigration was however accompanied by a much more significant discussion about *integration* (cf. Joppke and Morawska, 2003). For while new primary (labour) migration was officially not permitted from 1973 onwards, all the main parties recognised that those foreigners who were already resident in Germany would need to be integrated. The question of how this might be achieved, and especially the degree of cultural acclimatisation (or more formally, assimilation) that should be expected from Germany's non-national population, has given rise to an intense party political dispute. This question is particularly sensitive given the institutionalised patterns of marginalisation that had become apparent among non-nationals in Germany by the late 1990s: foreigners had higher unemployment rates, lower formal and practical levels of education and a lower socio-economic status (measured by incomes and access to living space) than Germans (Beauftragte der Bundesregierung, 2002; see also Table 5.1, p. 118). Such patterns are of course reflected in other European countries such as France, the Netherlands and the UK, but in Germany they are compounded by the lower levels of legal integration arising from the 'non-immigration' dogma. As the Appendix shows, there is a considerable gap between residence periods and the proportion of foreigners holding either secure residence titles or being granted German citizenship (see also Thränhardt, 2000: 150). Traditionally, Germany has had some of the lowest naturalisation rates anywhere in the EU.

In addition, as with so many areas of German politics, the past, and in particular the national-socialist past, casts an omnipresent shadow over contemporary German society. To put it neutrally, given Germany's past treatment of non-Germans, the status of immigrants in German society is a highly sensitive topic. Furthermore, the past has imbued Germany's unique constitutional guarantee of political asylum with a symbolism unmatched in other developed countries. Equally, given the international context of post-unification fears over renewed German nationalism, implicit or explicit accusations that Germany is 'racist' because of its *Ausländerpolitik* find substantial resonance and are closely scrutinised (e.g. Wilpert, 1993; *Independent*, 13 May 1998; *The Times*, 12 January 1999; Panayi, 2001; cf. Layton-Henry and Wilpert, 2003).

Ironically, for all this controversy, recent developments have underlined that Germany will quite simply need immigration in the coming decades (see Chapter 5). In common with other European countries, Germany's population is both shrinking in size (due to very low birth rates) and ageing. In 2000, a seminal comparative United Nations report calculated that the ratio between those in work supporting those who are not labour market active will halve between 1995 and 2050 (United Nations, 2000). This has existential implications for the country's social security system, which relies on cross-generational, pay-as-you-go transfers; already by 2020, demographic changes will put this under considerable strain. On top of this, Germany is experiencing both skilled and unskilled labour shortages, for instance in information technology. Even if working lives are increased and more family-friendly policies introduced, it is difficult to see how these demographic challenges can be met without at least some new immigration (see Münz, Seifert and Ulrich, 1997; Münz and Ulrich, 2000; Green, 2002; cf. Schmid, 2001).

At various times, all of these factors have contributed to the very passionate and polarised nature of the domestic political debate on the status and rights of foreigners over the years. Put simply, this has seen the parties of the Left, consisting of the Social-democratic Party of Germany (SPD), the ecologist Greens and the post-communist Party of Democratic Socialism (PDS),[2] together with the centrist and liberal Free Democratic Party (FDP), square off against the conservative Right, represented by the Christian Democratic Union (CDU) and its Bavarian sister party, the Christian Social Union (CSU).[3] Broadly speaking, the parties of the Left and Centre have promoted a rights-based view of membership and integration, while the CDU and CSU (hereafter CDU/CSU) have emphasised their desire to maintain what they perceive as Germany's cultural homogeneity.

While the respective positions of the parties on *Ausländerpolitik* have already been compared extensively elsewhere (Frey, 1982: 127–43; Knight and Kowalsky, 1991; Murray, 1994; Çelik, 1995; O'Brien, 1996), it is the nature and results of the conflict between them that form a central element of this book's argument. For one thing, there is actually more cross-party consensus in *Ausländerpolitik* than meets the eye; indeed the 1960s and 1970s were positively defined by such a consensus. As the subsequent chapters show, party conflict remains structured around the symbolic level of *Ausländerpolitik* and continues to be dominated by two questions: first, is Germany a country of immigration and second, to what extent should foreigners be expected to assimilate into German society? These disputes should not be trivialised in any way; indeed, they have had a considerable impact on both the content and timing of policy output. But despite these differences, one of the most remarkable aspects of *Ausländerpolitik* in Germany is how little an impact a change of government has had on policy output. Even when major policy revisions are undertaken, three of which will be discussed in greater detail in later chapters, the overall impact is often marginal, or, to borrow a term from Peter Katzenstein, 'incremental'.

Connected to this point is the final reason why this investigation is timely. In 1998, after sixteen years in office, the CDU/CSU–FDP government under Helmut Kohl was replaced by a new SPD–Green government under Gerhard Schröder. Not only was this change itself a first in German politics (Green, 1999), but its particular relevance for the discussion of *Ausländerpolitik* was that it brought the Greens, who over the years have been the most vociferous proponents of inclusive policies for foreigners, to national power for the first time. Accordingly, their first period in office from 1998 to 2002 saw two crucial legislative initiatives, first in citizenship policy and then in immigration policy, which promised to completely redefine the structures, aims and methods of this policy area. This book provides an ideal opportunity to examine the formulation, and fate, of these initiatives. As Chapters 3, 4 and 5 will show, the pressures for incremental change remain almost irresistibly strong in this policy area, irrespective of which parties are actually in power at national level.

Building a framework for analysis

The lens through which this book will examine *Ausländerpolitik* is that of policy-making, and the remainder of this introductory chapter is dedicated to outlining the models of policy-making and governance which will be employed throughout the subsequent analysis. Hitherto, this variable has received relatively little attention in studies of this particular policy area, with scholarly (and highly stimulating) treatises of Germany instead focusing on aspects such as history, law, the impact of the state and the role of liberalism (e.g. Brubaker, 1992; O'Brien, 1996; Joppke, 1999; Rubio-Marin, 2000).

Of these, Rogers Brubaker's 1992 eloquent comparison of French and German citizenship traditions and policies stands out as a particularly influential volume. His historically based analysis remains a yardstick in this area, even if some of his conclusions have come to be challenged by subsequent research (see for instance the outstanding analysis by Hagedorn, 2001). A central tenet of Brubaker's work is the notion that France and Germany's different citizenship policies are rooted in different traditions of national self-understanding. As he argues, 'France and Germany continue to define their citizenries in fundamentally different ways because they have been doing so for more than a century' (Brubaker, 1992: 186). However intuitively correct such a conclusion may seem, it does rest on two critical assumptions: that elites' understanding of German nationhood and citizenship has remained homogeneous in the late twentieth century and that the policy-making process is nothing more than a 'black box' which requires no further elucidation. Brubaker actually acknowledges this:

> I should emphasise that I am not trying to account for the fine details of particular policy outcomes. Clearly these depend on a host of factors unrelated to patterns of national self-understanding. The policy-making process is highly contingent. Yet if elite understandings of nationhood have little bearing on the timing or detailed content of legislative change, they do help explain the otherwise puzzling persistence of broadly different ways of defining the citizenry. They limit the universe of debate and make a fundamental restructuring of citizenship improbable. (Brubaker, 1992: 185)

This book will demonstrate that Brubaker's argument demands much greater precision. On the one hand, the notion of a prevailing elite consensus, especially over the symbolism of German citizenship, is difficult to sustain from the late 1970s onwards. On the other hand, this lack of consensus means that the policy-making process, far from determining simply 'fine details', actually plays a critical role in explaining policy output. Moreover, the role of timing is likely to be higher than credited by Brubaker: the subsequent chapters will argue that, in the case of *Ausländerpolitik*, exogenous factors such as the unification of Germany and endogenous factors such as the change of government in 1998 helped determine the overall value parameters within which legislative initiatives were formulated (Green, 2001a).

How, then, can the German policy-making process be characterised? What are its salient features and patterns of outcomes? A range of eminent contributions have helped develop a sophisticated and differentiated picture of the German polity and its outputs. For instance, West Germany's policy style has been described as seeking a 'rationalist consensus', in which negotiation rather than imposition is the norm (Dyson, 1982), and its economic policy has been characterised as a 'policy of the middle way' (Schmidt, 1987). In terms of institutional interactions, 'institutional pluralism' (Bulmer, 1989), the 'grand coalition state' (Schmidt, 1996, 2003) and German federalism's 'joint-decision trap' (Scharpf, 1988) have all become established terms in understanding public policy in Germany.

But arguably the most complete and significant characterisation of institutions and outcomes is Peter Katzenstein's study of 'semi-sovereignty' in West Germany, which has established itself as one of the most influential analyses of German politics in recent decades (Katzenstein, 1987). The central element of Katzenstein's hypothesis, which in this case refers to internal rather than external semisovereignty, is that power in (West) Germany is widely dispersed, explicitly in order to circumscribe central government's scope for action. This dispersal of power, combined with a strong moral imperative towards consensus in policy-making, is largely rooted in Germany's pre-1945 history, or what Manfred Schmidt (1989) describes as 'learning from catastrophes'.

For Katzenstein, the various policy actors in Germany's semisovereign state can be grouped under two broad headings: the decentralised state and centralised society. These two groups of actors interact within a highly formalised and extensive network, which is organised around three so-called 'nodes': political parties, cooperative federalism and parapublic institutions. The nodes are absolutely critical for the operation of semisovereignty, as it is through them that policy change is negotiated and implemented. Their interactions are structured in such a way that 'large scale departures from established policies [are] an improbable occurrence' (Katzenstein, 1987: 35), culminating in a tendency towards what Katzenstein calls 'incremental outcomes'. Katzenstein then goes on to illustrate this model using six different case studies of economic and social policy. Uniquely among studies of policy-making in Germany, he includes 'migrant labour', although his discussion is limited to the processes and effects of labour migration up to the mid-1980s. By focusing on dependant migration, citizenship and residence policy, this book both broadens out his analysis and extends it into the 1990s and the new millennium.

Since its publication, Katzenstein's model has been complemented by models from comparative politics, notably veto players' theory (Tsebelis, 1995, 2002). This concept has similarly been used to highlight the marked inability of the German federal government in cross-national comparison to impose policy decisions in an outright majoritarian manner (Schmidt, 2002). But the semisovereign model of governance remains unique in that it is rooted in a profound understanding of Germany and German politics which appreciates the impact of historical experience and the importance of norms in policy-making. In consequence, it remains highly relevant to German politics today.

Both as a result of its coherence and because of its initial coverage of immigration, this model, backed up by the analyses of other authors, is able to offer significant insights into the origins of policy outcomes in *Ausländerpolitik*. It is therefore worth examining its key features and arguments, including specific reference to the slightly unusual institutional arrangements in this policy sector, in more detail.

Decentralised state and centralised society

Let us first consider the nature of the decentralised state. Under this heading, Katzenstein (1987: 15–23) identifies four key elements. First, Germany's federal constitution, with first eleven and (after 1990) sixteen federal states (*Länder*), forms a highly visible and obvious limit on central government power. In terms of legislative competencies, this should certainly not be overstated. Over the course of the past fifty years, the federal level has made full use of its constitutional right to supersede *Länder* legislation in certain areas (the so-called *konkurrierende Gesetzgebung*, or 'competing legislative competencies'). Nonetheless, the *Länder* have still managed to retain an essential role in the political system, which is manifested in two key ways. On the one hand, the *Länder* have a collective direct input into federal policy-making via the upper chamber of parliament, the *Bundesrat*. On the other hand, Germany's Basic Law differentiates between the functions of formulation and implementation in federal domestic policy, with the latter role being assigned to the *Länder* in most areas. Crucially, even if a bill sponsored by the federal government amends only the executive competencies of the *Länder*, the *Bundesrat* exercises a right of veto, which currently applies to around 60 per cent of all bills, including most of those in the area of *Ausländerpolitik* (so-called 'consent laws').

Potentially, the *Länder* can thus exercise an important collective check on the federal government's scope for action, although this of course depends on mobilising enough votes to mount a blocking veto. In theory, this should be relatively simple, as consent laws require an absolute majority of the sixty-nine votes in the chamber to pass. This in turn means that abstentions, which is the default option when individual *Länder* coalition partners disagree over specific legislative proposals, effectively count as 'no' votes. Such disagreements are pre-programmed in *Länder* coalitions which cut across the government–opposition party divide at federal level – for instance, Baden-Württemberg's grand coalition between CDU and SPD from 1992 to 1996. With this type of coalition becoming more widespread after unification (details in Bräuninger and König, 1999: 218–19), abstentions have become more common in the *Bundesrat*. Hence, the total number of votes mustered by *Länder* with a similar political complexion to that of the federal government has usually fallen short of the necessary thirty-five to pass consent legislation (Schmidt, 2003: 58–60).[4] Indeed, there has been a lively debate in German political science since the 1970s over whether the opposition at federal level has been able to instrumentalise the *Bundesrat*'s characteristics as a veto point to frustrate the federal government's policy agenda (see Lehmbruch, 1976; Sturm, 1999; also Abromeit, 1992). While instances of organised blockade can certainly be found, the blocking minority has also not always been easy to mobilise, especially when the underlying tensions between the party political interests of federal politics and the heterogeneous territorial interests of *Länder* politics come into play (cf. Jeffery, 1999). On the contrary, the federal government has on occasion been able to exploit this tension and use 'divide-and-rule' tactics to ensure that its proposals were passed, as the Schröder government's tax reform in 2000 graphically illustrated (*Der Spiegel*, 17 July 2000).

But such occasions remain relatively rare and it is more the threat than the reality of veto which has tended to force both CDU- and SPD-led federal governments to negotiate with the respective opposition. Although the number of bills which is formally rejected by the *Bundesrat* remains very low (Renzsch, 1999; Rudzio, 2000: 326), the degree to which federal governments prefer 'non-decisions' over striking potentially wide-reaching compromises with the opposition parties remains difficult to gauge. Non-decisions are a well-established analytical tool in German politics and are defined thus:

> A non-decision ... is a decision that results in the suppression or thwarting of a latent or manifest challenge to the values and interests of the decision maker. To be more clearly explicit, non-decision-making is a means by which demands for change in the existing allocation of benefits and privileges in the community can be suffocated before they are even voiced; or kept covert; or killed to gain access to the relevant decision-making arena; or failing all these things, maimed or destroyed in the decision-implementing process. (Bachrach and Baratz, 1970: 7)

Certainly, as Chapters 3 and 4 will show, this option of 'non-decisions' has been a recurrent factor in *Ausländerpolitik*. For instance, the CDU/CSU–FDP federal government preferred this option over what it considered to be a sub-optimal outcome in citizenship policy between 1994 and 1998. Elsewhere, the spectre and indeed existence of hostile *Bundesrat* majorities has played a significant part in *Ausländerpolitik*: in key pieces of legislation passed in 1990 and 1999 (see Chapters 3 and 4, respectively), significant components of the final policy outcome can be attributed to the political composition of the *Bundesrat* at that time.

The second area of the decentralised state is the Federal Constitutional Court (*Bundesverfassungsgericht*). With its activist remit of competencies, it has exercised a strong influence on German policy-making over the decades. Its judgements have helped define the terms of debate in a whole range of structural and policy issues, including the division of power between the federation and the *Länder*, abortion rights and also *Ausländerpolitik*. As subsequent chapters will underline, from the 1970s onwards, the Court has repeatedly handed down rulings which have had major implications for policy outcome in this area (Joppke, 1999). The Court therefore represents a crucial constraint on government policy in this and other fields in German politics. At the same time, the importance of other courts should not be underestimated. This is especially true of the administrative courts, which play a central role in reviewing asylum decisions and thereby interpreting legal standards.

The third and fourth factors defining Germany's decentralised state are its strong tradition of bureaucratic independence and the relative lack of direct power of the federal chancellor. Katzenstein draws out both the strong hierarchical nature of the administration and the formal separation between the federal ministerial bureaucracy and the implementing level which, as already noted, is usually located within the *Länder*. As Katzenstein (1987: 22) argues, 'federal ministries lack experience in the details of policy implementation and tend to focus more on policy formulation'. Inevitably, this reliance on outside expertise for evaluation within the context of the policy cycle (Parsons, 1995: 77–81) creates mutual interdependence between federal ministries on the one hand and both interest groups and the *Länder* on the other. This pattern is reflected in *Ausländerpolitik*, in which the Federal Interior Ministry (*Bundesministerium des Innern*) has since the 1980s been the 'lead' portfolio, in accordance with the shift in policy emphasis towards asylum, family reunification and citizenship.

Finally, the formal power of the federal chancellor (*Bundeskanzler*) is limited compared to other countries (Helms, 2001) and is derived principally from his or her ability to set the general guidelines of policy (*Richtlinienkompetenz*). This means that individual ministers are independent in the political and practical leadership of their portfolios (the so-called *Ressortprinzip*). Of course, the chancellor has more scope for leadership in foreign and European policy (Paterson, 1998). But in domestic politics, including *Ausländerpolitik*, the chancellor's ability to set the guidelines for policy is in practice limited by two key factors. First, there is usually an information deficit resulting from the *Ressortprinzip*: even though the Federal Chancellery has developed into a formidable centre of expertise in its own right, it can rarely match the detailed policy expertise of the relevant lead ministry. Second, the mechanism of coalition politics at the federal level means that not all ministers will come from the same party as the chancellor. Indeed, for the Interior Ministry, this was the case throughout the duration of the SPD–FDP coalition from 1969 to 1982, during which time the FDP held the portfolio, and also up until 1989, when the minister came from the CSU. Even when the interior minister does come from the chancellor's party, as has been the case from 1989 onwards, the tendency for other coalition partners to lay down all aspects of the policy programme in some considerable detail in advance by means of a 'coalition treaty' has served to limit individual ministers' scope for action (Katzenstein, 1987: 22–3). In later chapters, this too will be shown to be a factor in determining *Ausländerpolitik*.

To these four factors identified by Katzenstein must be added one other element of the post-unification decentralised state: the impact of the EU. In Katzenstein's original text, the supranational level played no significant role, reflecting the fact that, at the time of his writing in the mid-1980s, the Single European Act (SEA) had not yet been signed and the single currency was still on the drawing board. However, by the turn of the millennium, the European dimension constituted a major source of domestic policy frameworks and initiatives (Schmidt, 2003: 94–5). *Ausländerpolitik* too has been affected. Already, the provisions for free movement in the Treaty of Rome (supplemented by the introduction of EU citizenship in the 1992 Treaty on European Union, TEU) have exempted EU nationals and their dependants from most immigration restrictions to Germany. This has created two classes of foreign residents, in the form of EU nationals and so-called third-country nationals, with real differences in the respective level of rights available to them. In addition, developments such as the 1985 Schengen Accord on the abolition of border controls, the 1990 Dublin Convention on asylum applications and, most importantly, the incorporation of immigration and asylum into the EU's so-called 'First Pillar' of supranational policy-making under the 1997 Treaty of Amsterdam have all served to further promote the process of policy integration (Geddes, 2000). Indeed, the Treaty of Amsterdam, confirmed by the 1999 Tampere

European Council, committed the EU to a common asylum and immigration policy by 2004. The legal impetus for Germany to develop effective anti-discrimination legislation has also come from the European level, in the form of Article 13 of the Amsterdam Treaty and two subsequent directives in 2000.

Early on, Germany was an enthusiastic supporter of Europeanisation in this field. Chancellor Kohl explicitly attempted to avoid the domestic quagmire of amending Germany's asylum legislation in 1991 and 1992 by seeking (albeit unsuccessfully) a political solution at the supranational level (Henson and Malhan, 1995). However, since domestic policy solutions helped Germany achieve the desired reduction in asylum seekers from 1993 onwards (see Chapter 4), its enthusiasm for EU-wide solutions on anything other than its own conditions has waned. A good example of this was Germany's insistence in 2001 that it should be allowed to impose a transitional period of up to seven years for free movement of labour following the accession of ten new states to the EU in 2004. In particular, successive interior ministers have argued that proposals from the European Commission on standards of recognition for asylum seekers and rules for family reunification would dilute Germany's own tough regulations. By the time of the federal election in 2002, relatively little progress had been made towards the goal of a harmonised immigration regime, notwithstanding some developments in the field of asylum policy and the jurisprudence of the European Court of Justice (ECJ), which had significantly improved the legal status of Turkish nationals under that country's 1963 Association Agreement with the EU. Neither had the two directives on anti-discrimination policy been implemented into national law. Overall, the degree of integration thus remains lower in immigration policy than in other sectors. With both non-EU immigration and residence policy, along with national citizenship, remaining almost wholly within the national remit of competencies during this book's period of analysis, the EU's impact in this area will not be accorded further detailed scrutiny.

In Katzenstein's model of semisovereign governance, the decentralised nature of state power is juxtaposed by the role and influence wielded by highly centralised and powerful societal interests, epitomised by trade unions and employers' organisations. These large 'class-based' interests are complemented by influential 'status groups', such as doctors' professional bodies and agricultural interests, who often have 'insider' status – that is, they are essential partners for the successful implementation of policy (Katzenstein, 1987: 23–30).

However, in *Ausländerpolitik*, societal interests are structured somewhat differently. Even though the usual array of social actors is present, encompassing unions, churches and their associated, publicly funded welfare organisations (Puskeppeleit and Thränhardt, 1990), their scope and influence is different than in other areas. This has two reasons. First, their role as 'insider' groups from the era of organised labour migration has eroded with the post-1973 shift in immigration policy towards the more regulatory issues of family reunification, asylum and citizenship. Second, even when societal interests were involved, they did not have the same degree of influence as for instance the pharmacists' lobby did on health policy, for one simple reason: in no case was any of the groups active in this field solely devoted to foreigners' interests. In fact, unions, churches and welfare organisations have all had other, frequently more important clienteles than foreigners. What is more, for many years their interest representation, while noble in its intentions, has unmistakably smacked of paternalism. For instance, even though foreign workers have long been more highly unionised than Germans, it was not until 1992 that a Turkish union member was elected to the executive of the metalworkers' union IG Metall (MAGS, 1994a: 90–3).

At the same time, the organisation of foreigners themselves remains fragmented. While foreigners are allowed to join political parties (with the exception of the CSU, which permits only EU nationals as members), they are by law forbidden to form the majority of the membership. So far, there have been only individual instances of parliamentarians of non-German origin. Moreover, where foreigners have organised themselves into societies and private interest groups, these have historically tended to be nationality-based (Decker, 1982: 106–50; Zentrum für Türkeistudien, 1994: 331–90), thereby underlining and simultaneously entrenching the (often overlooked) ethnic and cultural heterogeneity of Germany's immigrant and non-national population.

In recent years, there has been a concerted attempt to involve foreigners in local government via consultative committees (*Ausländerbeiräte*). Indeed, as non-EU nationals do not and cannot have the right to vote at local level (see pp. 56–7), this format is one of the few methods of political participation open to them. Such *Ausländerbeiräte* have become commonplace in municipalities of all sizes since the early 1970s, and vary considerably in their structure, for instance in the form of democratic legitimisation (whether by election or appointment), in the balance between German and foreign members of the committee and

in the extent to which national quotas are employed to prevent domi-
nation of the committee by the largest nationality (usually Turks)
(Decker, 1982: 57–8; Bommes, 1991; MAGS, 1994b). The states of
Hesse, North Rhine-Westphalia and Lower Saxony were the first to
make large-scale use of these institutions and to include them in their
respective local government constitutions (*Gemeindeordnungen*), although it was not until 1998 that a *Bundesausländerbeirat* at federal
level could be formed.

Where these committees do exist, they are often hampered by their
focus on local matters, by the tendency towards an extremely low electoral
turnout, often under 10 per cent (MAGS, 1994b: 215–18; Beauftragte
der Bundesregierung, 2002: 170–1), which obviously reduces their democratic legitimacy, and by the fact that their status is almost entirely
consultative. Naturally, it is a moot point to what extent one factor
influences the other, but ultimately, the impact of *Ausländerbeiräte* has
been very low (cf. Hoffmann, 2002).

Overall, it is fair to conclude that direct interest representation of
non-nationals has so far been fragmented, difficult and largely unsuccessful. Their membership in political parties remains possible but
unusual, while the unions have been slow to integrate their considerable
foreign membership fully into their leadership structures. Other attempts to develop dedicated structures of interest representation have,
so far, gone little further than tokenism. With the key political right of
suffrage available only to Germans (and EU nationals at local and
European level), the promotion of foreigners' interests in Germany
remains dependent on the goodwill of other societal actors. Unfortunately for foreigners, such actors often have broader agendas than solely
focusing on their welfare.

The nodes of the network

As noted, the interaction between the actors of the decentralised state
and centralised society is structured within a range of so-called 'nodes'
of the policy network, of which Katzenstein singles out three as especially
important: political parties, parapublic institutions and cooperative
federalism. Of these, political parties are arguably the most significant:
not only is their role in interest mediation constitutionally acknowledged
but it is also well funded via the public purse. In particular, the
parliamentary parties (*Fraktionen*) have developed into formidable political power bases in their own right. As in the US Congress, the

leadership of the parties in the legislature represents one of the most powerful positions in German politics.

For the purposes of understanding *Ausländerpolitik*, we must differentiate between the large parties (CDU/CSU and SPD) and the smaller parties (FDP and Greens) who in various combinations have made up every federal government in Germany since 1961. On the one hand, the CDU/CSU and SPD cannot simply be labelled as large parties grounded solely in their respective class-based milieux. Indeed, both have consciously defined themselves as so-called *Volksparteien* ('people's parties'), with relatively large memberships and broad electoral bases bridging the main traditional electoral cleavages of class and religion. Their broad electoral appeal is mirrored in the composition of their membership (Katzenstein, 1987: 39) which, in terms of *Ausländerpolitik*, means both that the rights-based approach normally associated with the SPD is also represented within the CDU/CSU, and that the latter party's emphasis on German cultural homogeneity also finds limited resonance within the SPD. This is a particular important characteristic of party politics in Germany, which will be seen to play a major role in debates in the 1980s and 1990s (see Chapters 3 and 4).

On the other hand, the smaller FDP and Greens, who have tended to pursue a more consistent rights-based line, derive their influence within this node of the network from the predominance of coalition politics produced by Germany's proportional electoral system. The principal beneficiary of this trend has been the FDP, which managed to stay in government continuously from 1969 to 1998 (discounting a negligible break of two weeks in September 1982), first with the SPD from 1969 to 1982, and then with the CDU/CSU until 1998. Its pivotal role as a potential coalition partner for either of the two *Volksparteien* in a 'triangular' party system (Pappi, 1984) has cemented its function as a centripetal influence on policy, which in turn has helped limit the effects of changes in the party composition of government (Katzenstein, 1987; Schmidt, 1987, 1989; Webber, 1992).

Of course, these dynamics have changed somewhat since the entry of the Greens into the federal parliament (*Bundestag*) at the 1983 federal election. In most issues, including *Ausländerpolitik*, the Greens have been situated to the left of the SPD (cf. Lees, 2000); in consequence, the SPD has been in the role of providing the centripetal influence since the two parties took power after the 1998 election. Nonetheless, both the *Ressortprinzip* and the practice of formulating detailed coalition treaties, as already noted, tend to furnish the junior partner, regardless of its ideological complexion, with a formal power which should not underestimated.

The second important node for understanding *Ausländerpolitik* is parapublic institutions, whose function it is to depoliticise controversial policy fields by turning them into areas of technical and administrative expertise. As Katzenstein writes, 'Parapublic institutions act like political shock-absorbers. They induce political stability both directly and indirectly. They tend to limit political controversies in the process of policy implementation. And they limit the scope of policy initiatives' (Katzenstein, 1987: 58).

The parapublic institution *par excellence* was, of course, the politically independent *Bundesbank* which, as guardian over the stability of Europe's largest currency, exercised significant power both within Germany and, indirectly, in other EU member-states. Katzenstein identifies a range of parapublic institutions in the field of *Ausländerpolitik*, principally the Federal Labour Office (*Bundesanstalt für Arbeit*, BA), and the four main private and Church welfare associations (Katzenstein, 1987: 225–6). Although parapublic institutions played a major role in policy management during the period of labour migration, their input ended once *Ausländerpolitik* evolved in the late 1970s to focus on asylum, family reunification and citizenship. Although this new policy focus brought the Federal Office for the Recognition of Foreign Refugees (*Bundesamt für die Anerkennung ausländischer Flüchtlinge*, BAFl) into play, its role was strictly limited to actually assessing the validity of asylum applications, and was hence excluded from the much more controversial aspects of asylum policy. Therefore, from the early 1980s onwards, a gap had emerged in the institutional configuration of this policy field. The question of how this came to be filled by political parties will be central to the discussion in Chapters 3, 4 and 5.

Finally, the structures of cooperative federalism play a central role in the question of turning policy into practice. For one thing, the strict division of responsibilities between formulation at the federal level and implementation at the sub-national level has necessitated a complex web of both horizontal (between the individual *Länder*) and vertical (between the *Länder* and the federation) coordinating mechanisms, in order to ensure some degree of similarity across the *Länder* in terms of policy outcomes (Leonardy, 1991). Yet despite these mechanisms, and the tendency towards formulating highly detailed primary and secondary legislation, unified outcomes in Germany are by no means guaranteed. Naturalisation and dual citizenship policy is an excellent example of this. As Hagedorn (2001: 151–62) shows, the proportion of non-nationals naturalised each year (the so-called 'naturalisation rate') has varied considerably between the *Länder*, with Bavaria especially standing out as particularly restrictive. However, while acknowledging the specificities of the Bavarian case, Hagedorn refutes the notion that this variation is *a priori* due to the party political leadership of a *Land*, noting that different administrative capacities offer a far more plausible explanation (see also Chapter 4).

The second implication of the division of labour between federal and sub-national levels is that territorial interests tend to be at least influenced by budgetary considerations, especially when the costs for proposed policy measures are borne by the *Länder*. This is certainly the case in *Ausländerpolitik* and especially in asylum policy, where the *Länder* are responsible for accommodating asylum seekers. In consequence, they have long supported restrictive measures aimed at reducing applications and thereby easing pressure on their budgets. The issues of *Ausländerpolitik* can therefore also constitute a source of the tensions between territorial and political interests outlined above.

One other institution deserves mention. The government's own Commissioner for Foreigners' Affairs (*Beauftragte der Bundesregierung für Ausländerfragen*) has played a visible, albeit often fruitless role in *Ausländerpolitik* since the office was established in 1978. The position of the office is certainly awkward: underresourced and located in the relatively marginal Federal Labour Ministry until 2002, it has had only a consultative role in the policy-making process, and as such is strictly speaking not a parapublic institution. Nonetheless, its four incumbents, helped by the office's high public profile, have still occasionally been able to influence government policy (Geiß, 2001).

Germany's incremental policy outcomes

Katzenstein's model of semisovereign governance thus neatly captures the diversity of institutions and actors which populate the policy-making arena in Germany. But it is his characterisation of the resulting policy outcomes as 'incremental' which is absolutely crucial for understanding *Ausländerpolitik*. For the purposes of this book, policy outcomes are therefore not simply conceived of as changes in legislation, but as the effects that these changes produce.

For Katzenstein, incremental outcomes arise from the patterns of

interaction between a decentralised state and centralised societal interests, patterns which are themselves conditioned by the normative pursuit
of cooperation and consensus in policy-making. He goes on to stress
that incremental change is a common factor for all federal governments:
'although the composition of government matters in policy and politics,
incremental policy changes are the parties' typical response to the
constraints of coalition governments as well as to their own internal
organisation' (Katzenstein, 1987: 42). He thereby underlines the role of
the *Volksparteien* themselves as a forum for compromise. At the same
time, Katzenstein emphasises that incremental change does not equate
to an 'incapacity to change' (Katzenstein, 1987: 350). Indeed, Manfred
Schmidt emphasises the German political system's ability to produce
change when needed, citing the 'big bang' approach to unification, which
produced a number of significant policy changes in the early 1990s
(Schmidt, 2003: 239).

   Although Katzenstein's emphasis on incremental policy change is
convincing, other authors in parallel emphasise the importance of 'path
dependency' for understanding policy change in Germany. Peters (1999:
63), drawing on Krasner (1984), defines this concept as follows: 'When
a government programme or organisation embarks upon a path there
is an inertial tendency for those initial policy choices to persist. That
path may be altered, but it requires a good deal of political pressure to
produce that change.'

   This phenomenon has long been identified in German public policy.
Already in 1981, Gordon Smith concluded that

> Once policies have been adopted there is strong pressure to maintain
> them, not only on the part of the government but also as an implied
> constraint on the opposition. In consequence, the political system is geared
> to making only gradual changes of course in any field of policy and putting
> stress on the virtue of continuity. (Smith, 1981: 174)

By contrast, Sturm considers that incrementalism is based on an underlying desire to maintain social and political stability, arguing that it is
a normative emphasis on rationalism which precludes radical changes:
'If Germany got it right in principle at the beginning, policy-making
afterwards only means adjusting to the changing social and political
environment. Policy-making does not *a priori* include the possibility of
a fresh start' (Sturm, 1996: 120).

   As subsequent chapters will show, the dynamics of path dependency,
already identified by authors such as Hansen (2000) and Longhurst

(2003) in the case of the UK's citizenship policy and Germany's security policy, respectively, are also an important factor in understanding policy outcomes in *Ausländerpolitik*.

The structure of the book

The preceding analysis has sought to establish the intellectual rationale for the following chronological analysis of *Ausländerpolitik* in Germany. This is based around a number of dimensions. The size, diversity and historical context of immigration are singular in Germany; likewise, the political denial of Germany as a country of immigration has been unique compared to most other countries. At the same time, immigration remains a potent political and electoral issue in German politics. Explaining why policy outcomes are what they are is therefore extremely important.

Yet as noted, scholarly analyses of this complex policy area have hitherto paid little attention to the role of the policy-making process in accounting for these outcomes. It is this gap which this study seeks to fill. To this end, Katzenstein's semisovereign model of governance is particularly helpful. Within a consensus-oriented environment, it identifies party political, constitutional, sub-national and formal political constraints on a federal government's ability to implement anything other than incremental changes to the (path-dependent) initial policy choices. Even though it was originally published in 1987, the semisovereign model of governance remains a powerful analytical tool, and most of its features remain clearly visible throughout German politics today.

The remaining four chapters of this book and the conclusion (Chapter 6) will build on Katzenstein's initial analysis of migrant labour policy to show how these characteristics of policy-making have impacted on outcomes from the 1980s onwards. They will show how the failure of policy evolution to keep pace with the societal reality of immigration helped create ever-stronger pressures for more radical and wholesale policy reform. But they will also show how various actors have combined within their own institutional logic to produce a policy which has, for better or for worse, been stable. The chapters thus tell the story of how a country's political class has struggled over decades to adapt to immigration and its resulting impact on domestic society.

The story begins in Chapter 2, which identifies the sources of path

dependency in the three main policy areas of this book. It first summarises the development of German citizenship from the early
nineteenth century through to the early 1950s and then traces the
definition of the frameworks for residence, family reunification and
naturalisation policy from the emergence of labour migration from 1955
through to the change of government in 1982. By this time, serious
differences had developed between the parties in their conceptions of
Ausländerpolitik, and the following three chapters show how, against
this background, the semisovereign model of governance can account
for policy outcomes. Each chapter covers a specific period of time and
is centred around a detailed case study of a major legislative initiative
in this area, as well as contextualising the respective general issues in
Ausländerpolitik. Thus Chapter 3 looks at the first real attempts to
change this path dependency during the 1980s, focusing on the reform
of the 1965 *Ausländergesetz* (literally, 'Foreigners' Law'). Chapter 4
examines the period from 1990 to 1999 and concentrates on the reform
of citizenship, first under the Kohl government until 1998, and then
under the SPD–Green government from 1998 onwards. Chapter 5
discusses the issues and processes surrounding the introduction of a
full-scale immigration law (*Zuwanderungsgesetz*) between 2000 and
2002.

   Together, these three case studies will stake out all the main developments in *Ausländerpolitik* over some twenty years, to include key
elements of asylum and ethnic German policy as well as a more detailed
examination of family reunification, residence and citizenship policy.
As the *Ausländergesetz*, the reform of citizenship and the debate over
the *Zuwanderungsgesetz* constitute not just three of the main issues in
Ausländerpolitik since 1982, but also three of the most important and
contentious items on the entire domestic policy agenda over that period,
the case studies can thereby provide a very clear sense of the nature of
governance in this area.

   In addition to providing conclusions following each case study, in
Chapter 6 the book undertakes an overall evaluation of the relationship
between semisovereignty and *Ausländerpolitik* from three perspectives.
First, how well does semisovereignty help to explain outcomes in
Ausländerpolitik? Second, how does *Ausländerpolitik* shape our understanding of semisovereign governance in Germany? Lastly, is
semisovereignty capable of providing answers to the policy challenges
posed by immigration?

Notes

1 Although precise numbers are difficult to establish, the Commissioner for Foreigners' Affairs estimated that around 1.1 million refugee-related persons and dependants were living in Germany in 2001 (Beauftragte der Bundesregierung, 2002).

2 The Greens' official name is *Bündnis 90/Die Grünen*, but the shorter anglicised version will be preferred in this book. The PDS is the successor party to the Socialist Unity Party of Germany (SED), which ruled the GDR from 1949 to 1990.

3 The two parties are formally independent of each other, but form a joint group (*Fraktion*) in the *Bundestag*. The CDU does not stand for election in Bavaria and the CSU does not campaign on a national platform. Throughout this book, they will be considered as one party, except where their differentiation is necessary for the precision of the argument.

4 The sixty-nine votes are weighted between *Länder* on the basis of population and range from six each for the four largest *Länder* (Bavaria, North Rhine-Westphalia, Baden-Württemberg and Lower Saxony) to three each for the small states of Saarland, Bremen, Hamburg and Mecklenburg-Western Pomerania. Prior to unification, there were a total of forty-two votes in the *Bundesrat*.

2

Setting the parameters of *Ausländerpolitik*

As Chapter 1 has shown, *Ausländerpolitik* is a policy area of considerable complexity, in both its formal structures and dimensions, and in its social and political effects on Germany. The aim of this chapter is to answer the question of why policy in the three principal sub-areas under scrutiny in this book (residence, citizenship and family reunification policy) operates with path dependency dynamics. To this end, it will be necessary to go back to the roots of *Ausländerpolitik* in 1955, the year in which organised labour migration to West Germany began. Even though immigration in fact has a much longer history, stretching back to the Second Empire (Brubaker, 1992: 114–37) and including large numbers of ethnic German refugees after 1945, the beginning of non-ethnic German immigration in 1955 provides the ideal point from which to consider *Ausländerpolitik*. The political responses to this labour migration, and in particular to the consequences of its suspension after 1973, provide key pointers as to why path dependency dynamics in combination with semisovereign structures prevented the necessary evolution of policy in the 1980s and 1990s. Already, several of the key characteristics of policy-making identified in Chapter 1 will become apparent during this chapter, including the tendency towards consensus politics, the input of the Constitutional Court and the dynamics of cooperative federalism.

Together with Chapter 3, this chapter will also highlight a subsidiary aspect of politics in this area which has had important effects for policy outcome. So far, it has been shown how *Ausländerpolitik* is effectively an 'umbrella term' to describe a series of discrete policy areas, which in their substance are only tangentially connected. Yet as this chapter will illustrate, the need to tread carefully by making precise differentiation has rarely been heeded by politicians and political parties alike, who have with regularity preferred to tar all foreigners with the same brush. As a result, there has been an element of 'spillover' from individual components to other essentially unrelated areas of *Ausländerpolitik*, which has affected policy outcomes throughout the sector.

As the main focus of this and subsequent chapters is on residence, citizenship and family reunification policy, the issues of ethnic German immigration and asylum will be discussed in broad terms only. First, though, the chapter begins by sketching out the development of German citizenship from the early nineteenth century onwards, which is critical for understanding why this became such a controversial issue in the 1980s and 1990s.

The traditions of German citizenship

As in other countries, the development of Germany's conception of citizenship is closely related to its historical development as a nation-state. Whereas France and Britain were forging ahead with the creation of modern democracies from the late eighteenth century onwards, Germany remained a politically fragmented assortment of minor kingdoms, princedoms and dukedoms. By the time unification was finally achieved in 1871, Germany was, in every sense, the 'belated nation' (Plessner, 1959).

The origins of Germany's notion of citizenship go back to the late eighteenth century, when German romantic intellectuals began to distance themselves from France by accentuating cultural differences, in particular language, as French was widely spoken at the Prussian court. When the Congress of Vienna in 1815, which regulated the new, post-Napoleonic European political order, failed to create a united German political entity, such intellectuals 'looked increasingly to the formation of a cultural cohesion among their people, rather than to a political unity which seemed distant' (Mosse, 1964: 2–3). The quest for unity thus embodied the search for national destiny, which occupied the minds of romanticist writers and intellectuals such as Herder, Fichte and, on a more popular level, the Brothers Grimm.

The ideology of unification and national destiny was based heavily on an esoteric, almost mystical conception of the German people, or *Volk*. George Mosse defines this term as follows:

To German thinkers ever since the birth of German romanticism in the

late eighteenth century, 'Volk' signified the union of a group of people
with a transcendental 'essence' ... [which represents] the source of [man's]
creativity, his depth of feeling, his individuality and his unity with other
members of the Volk. (Mosse, 1964: 4)

While, in a modern-day context, Hailbronner acknowledges Germany's
'understanding of nationhood as an ethnic and cultural community'
(Hailbronner, 1989: 74), this had a far wider significance in the eyes of
the German romantic movement. The German *Volk* was genetically
distinct and biologically 'alive', and its members formed a *Schicksalsge-
meinschaft*, literally a 'community of common destiny'. Thus Münch
(1996: 21) concludes that 'the *Volk* was not simply conceived of as a
people but as a community of common blood, the roots of which had
to be traced back to its biological ancestors'.

Citizenship in unified Germany, 1871–1945

Perhaps inevitably, the eventual unification of Germany under the
leadership of Prussia failed to live up to its billing as the apogee of
national destiny. For when it finally came, 'it seemed prosaic, concerned
with everyday problems, whereas the movement toward that unity had
been highly idealistic and indeed utopian' (Mosse, 1964: 3–4). Moreover,
by not encompassing Austria, the community of the *Volk* remained split
between the two Germanic countries (the so-called *kleindeutsche Lösung*). Wilhelmine Germany also contained substantial Polish and
Danish minorities. Thus unified Germany was in many ways an 'in-
complete nation-state' during whose entire existence 'the tension
between the concept of Germans as citizens of a territorial state and
members of a *Volk* remained unresolved' (Pulzer, 1996: 304–5). In many
ways, unified Germany represented an artificial construct which needed
to engender its own 'national' identity among its subjects (Breuilly,
1992: 12–14).

The development of German citizenship law up to 1913 fully bears
out the contradictory nature of cultural imperatives and political realities
of this period. As Brubaker notes, 'before 1913 German citizenship was
internally inconsistent. It stood between two models – an older model
of the citizenry as a territorial community and a newer model of the
citizenry as a community of descent' (Brubaker, 1992: 115). This contradiction arises from the formal dominance of *ius domicili*, the principle
of residence, as the method of ascription among most German states
prior to 1842. Only gradually did *ius sanguinis*, the principle of descent,

come to replace *ius domicili*, which continued to operate at least implicitly in many states up to 1870 (Fahrmeier, 1997). The incremental increase in *ius sanguinis* bears evidence of the gradual rise of ethnonational (*völkisch*) ideology as the underlying definition of membership of the German people. If the *Volk* is a genetic, biological entity, then it is only logical that membership of it may be transferred only via the blood, the purity of which may best be maintained through *ius sanguinis* (Hoffmann, 1992: 102).

Legally, *ius sanguinis* as the principle of ascription was first formulated in the Bavarian citizenship edict of 26 May 1818 and broke through to more general acceptance when it was incorporated into the Prussian citizenship law of 31 December 1842. By the time it was included in the first *Reich* law of 1 June 1870 and finally in the *Reichs- und Staatsangehörigkeitsgesetz* (RuStAG) of 22 July 1913, the purity of the *Volk* had become an accepted political goal, at least for the nationalist mainstream. For instance, a national liberal *Reichstag* deputy declared on 23 February 1912, during the deliberations on the RuStAG, that 'the ... aim of this law is to prevent foreigners who would not be welcome here from becoming Germans; non-German blood is to be prevented from being assimilated into the German Fatherland' (quoted in *Frankfurter Rundschau*, 10 February 1999).

Politically, too, these three laws mirrored the development of German society. The 1870 law still based *Reich* citizenship on membership of one of Germany's constituent states, but provided that Germans who lived abroad for ten years automatically lost their citizenship, a condition that affected the millions of Germans who had emigrated to the United States in the 1880s and 1890s. As *völkisch* ideas gained in respectability during the Wilhelmine era, this particular provision became anathema to groups such as the Pan-German league, who demanded a more overtly national approach to citizenship (Brubaker, 1992: 116). Moreover, imperial Germany's booming economy had seen the number of foreigners treble between 1890 and 1910. In reply, after no less than fifteen years of discussion, the RuStAG was passed in 1913. It created Germany's first true national citizenship, prescribing *ius sanguinis* as the sole method of ascription of citizenship at birth, while removing the stipulation of loss of nationality for expatriates.[1] In its essence, it was to remain unchanged for over eighty-five years.

In many ways, the most remarkable thing about German citizenship is not that it was defined according to ethnonational principles in 1913: this merely reflected the priorities of the time, and it would be unfair to assume that Germany was alone in adopting such a line. What is remarkable is the fact that this definition should persist for so long. The explanation for this continuity lies in the tragic consequences of National-Socialism and the resulting division of Germany after 1945. Not only did the RuStAG remain in force during the ill-fated experiment of the Weimar Republic, but also under Nazi rule, as its ethnocultural definition of German membership was perfectly suited to the Third Reich's goals. Accordingly, the Nazis simply supplemented the RuStAG with their own laws, announced at Nuremberg in 1935. These sought not only to prevent non-Germans from becoming citizens (as the Wilhelmine political aim had been), but also to deprive existing (Jewish) citizens of their rights.

The transformation of the RuStAG into post-war German citizenship

Ironically, one of the main results of the defeat of Nazi Germany was that the expulsions of Germans from former eastern territories in the immediate post-war years led to a greater degree of ethnic and cultural homogeneity within the territorial boundaries of the German state than had been the case at any time previously in Germany's history (Katzenstein, 1987: 12–15). Yet curiously, while total defeat in 1945 represented a break with the past in many respects, this was not the case for German citizenship:

> The collapse of the Third Reich and the discrediting of *völkisch* ideology might have been expected to discredit German self-understanding as an ethnocultural nation as well. Instead, the peculiar circumstances of the immediate post-war period – the collapse of the state, the massive expulsion of ethnic Germans from Eastern Europe and the Soviet Union, and the imposed division of Germany – reinforced and powerfully relegitimated that self-understanding. (Brubaker, 1992: 168)

This paradox arose because of the Federal Republic's definition of citizenship in Article 116 of the Basic Law, which defined 'Germans' (but notably not West Germans) in two ways:

- Anyone who possessed German citizenship

- Anyone who had been admitted to the territory of the German Reich within the frontiers of 31 December 1937 as a refugee or expellee of German ethnic origin (*deutscher Volkszugehöriger*) or as their spouse or descendant.

By re-emphasising the ethnocultural nature of German citizenship in its constitution, West Germany deliberately fell back on the RuStAG and *ius sanguinis* for the basis of its citizenship (Brubaker, 1992: 168–71). This had two main reasons. First, the founding fathers of the Federal Republic were at pains not to legitimise the *de facto* partition of Germany. By maintaining German citizenship in terms of the RuStAG, Konrad Adenauer, West Germany's first chancellor, was able to undermine the newly founded German Democratic Republic (GDR) by recognising neither it nor its citizenship. West Germany's claim to represent all Germans (*Alleinvertretungsanspruch*) could be made credible only if its definition of citizenship also included all inhabitants of the GDR, which the 1913 law, with its provision that German citizenship was inherited, did. Thus under West German law, all East German citizens effectively kept their German citizenship and passed it on to their descendants, regardless of the fact that the GDR later established its own citizenship.

Second, the idea that citizenship was inherited, even in territories no longer belonging to Germany, formed the most important of the legal constructs which enabled West Germany to take in the millions of refugees expelled from Germany's former eastern territories after the end of the war. Crucially, this right of return for ethnic Germans was extended in the 1953 *Bundesvertriebenen- und Flüchtlingsgesetz* (BVFG) to include those living in territories which had never been German, including the Soviet Union and China. As most members of this group were descendants of people who had emigrated from Germany centuries earlier, this law further strengthened the ethnic bias of German citizenship. Throughout the division of Germany, a steady stream of ethnic Germans was able to claim entry and citizenship under this banner, which increased to a flood around the time of the collapse of Communism (see Chapter 4).

The beginnings of non-ethnic German migration: the guestworker phase, 1955–73

This, then, was the background of national self-definition against which non-ethnic German migration began in 1955. Its origins may be traced back to the spectacular post-war economic miracle that West Germany experienced during the 1950s. With annual real GDP growth averaging 8.2 per cent between 1950 and 1960, work was plentiful, and by 1960 the economy had reached full employment (Herbert, 2001: 194–5). Yet already by 1955 agriculture was bemoaning a severe shortage of labour, and the danger of a more general labour shortage in industry was looming increasingly large. In the business-friendly climate of the 1950s, the question of easing these inflationary pressures on the domestic labour market thus became a political priority. But the problem remained of where such extra labour was to come from: the flows of GDR citizens and post-war refugees from Germany's former eastern territories had already been absorbed into the labour market, and the construction of the Berlin Wall in 1961 was to cut off the former as a source of labour altogether. The situation was further compounded from 1955 onwards, when the rearmament of West Germany resulted in the loss of over 500,000 men from the labour market to the new armed forces, the *Bundeswehr* (Bischoff and Teubner, 1992: 34).

It was Ludwig Erhard, West Germany's legendary Economics Minister, who first proposed the idea of recruiting labour on a temporary basis from the less developed countries of southern Europe to make up this shortfall. Agriculture was the first sector to benefit, and the first Italian farm labourers arrived in Baden-Württemberg in the summer of 1955. This encouraged the federal government to sign a signed a formal recruitment treaty with Italy on 20 December 1955, which permitted the Federal Labour Office to open recruitment offices and act on behalf of German industry. Further such treaties were signed in 1960 with Spain and Greece, and with Turkey (1961), Morocco (1963), Portugal (1964), Tunisia (1965) and Yugoslavia (1968).[2]

Initially, recruitment of *Gastarbeiter* (literally, 'guestworkers') was small-scale. In 1960, there were still only around 690,000 foreigners in West Germany, of which 280,000, mostly guestworkers, were in tax-paying employment (*sozialversicherungspflichtige Beschäftigung*).[3] However, as the economy grew, and with it the demand for cheap labour, recruitment intensified during the 1960s, and by 1964 the one-millionth guestworker had arrived in the country. Although recruitment was reduced during the first post-war recession in 1966 and 1967, the renewed economic upswing from 1968 onwards resulted in the most vigorous drive for foreign labour yet. Between 1968 and 1972, the number of foreigners in tax-paying employment in West Germany more than doubled from 1 million to 2.3 million; in relative terms, this represented an increase from 52 per cent of non-national residents to an all-time high of 66 per cent. The countries of origin changed too: whereas Greeks and Italians had dominated in the early years, it was

Turkish guestworkers who formed the largest single group from the late 1960s onwards.[4]

Politically, the three main parties were right behind guestworker recruitment. Although the extreme-right National-democratic Party of Germany (NPD) had politicised the issue with some electoral success between 1966 and 1969, the policy was continued despite the changes in governmental composition in 1961, 1966 and 1969.[5] Guestworkers were considered by all concerned to be a purely temporary measure to alleviate labour market shortages. Their entire existence was seen solely from this perspective, as the following excerpt from a West German newspaper from 1968 illustrates:

> Guestworkers are in demand again by German industry and according to the Federal Labour Office, Turks are particularly popular. This is why they are hardest to obtain. Firms have to wait ten weeks just for auxiliary workers ... All in all, the market for guestworkers is extremely buoyant this summer. Italians are practically sold out, except for a small number of artisans. (Quoted in Meier-Braun, 1995: 16)

In order to minimise costs for society (which would arise in the form of schools, housing and health care provision for permanent immigrants and their dependants), the Federal Labour Office usually favoured young, single men, who were hired to work in German firms for two to three years. Once in Germany, they would often live in company-owned hostels, with little contact to the indigenous population (von Oswald and Schmidt, 1999). With the expiry of their contract, the intention was that guestworkers would return to their home countries, to be replaced by fresh labourers (Bade, 1994). As a result, this *modus operandi* soon became known as the 'principle of rotation' (*Rotationsprinzip*).

Overall, this principle was very successful. Klaus Bade calculates that, between 1955 and 1973, a total of 14 million guestworkers came to West Germany, of which 11 million (almost 80 per cent) returned to their home countries (Bade, 1994: 54). But it soon became apparent that both employers and unions found the system unsatisfactory (Bischoff and Teubner, 1992: 46–7). Many employers wanted to avoid the costs of having to train a large number of workers afresh every few years and the unions wanted to prevent foreign labour from undercutting the German workforce through short-term (and thereby cheaper) contracts. With both business and labour interests favouring a regularisation of foreign labour, albeit for different reasons, guestworkers increasingly received permanent contracts, which in turn meant that the authorities began to renew both residence and work permits more regularly. This gradually transformed a largely temporary workforce into a more permanent addition to the labour market, and the longer-term perspective provided by unlimited contracts and permits encouraged foreign workers to bring their families over to West Germany. Soon, the number of children born to foreign parents began to rise, although, because of the RuStAG's exclusive reliance on *ius sanguinis*, they remained foreign nationals at birth.

Instituting a legal framework: the 1965 *Ausländergesetz*

Remarkably, no formal legal framework for foreigners' residence existed before 1965, even though by then the recruitment of guestworkers was already in its tenth year and over 1 million foreigners were working in West German factories. Foreign labour was accepted by the parties, the unions and employers as essential for the good health of the West German economy, which precluded the need for a substantive political debate (Katzenstein, 1987: 213, 215). Among the wider public too, indifference reigned supreme (Schönwalder, 1996: 163).

It is with some justification, therefore, that the legal commentator Fritz Franz noted that 'legislation governing foreigners' residence lay in deep hibernation' (Franz, 1992: 154). Indeed, the only legal instrument governing the residence of foreigners in West Germany was the Nazi-enacted *Ausländerpolizeiverordnung* (APVO) of 22 April 1938, a police decree which had been put back onto the statute books in 1951. Accordingly, its provisions were dictated by the imperatives of the Third Reich: Section 1 stated that 'residence of foreigners will only be permitted if their character and reason for residence in the Reich guarantees that they are worthy of the hospitality extended towards them'.

Apart from the inevitable embarrassment of relying on a decree passed by one of the most racist regimes in history to regulate the residence of non-nationals, the APVO was considered to be technically deficient, and so *Land* and local authorities began to lobby for a more comprehensive regulatory instrument (Schönwalder, 1999). On 28 September 1962, after some internal discussion, the government introduced a bill into parliament. Its passage through the *Bundestag* epitomised the high normative emphasis on consensus, based around the perceived rationally best solution, that existed at this time (de Haan, 1990: 330–2; Franz, 1990: 3).

Astonishingly, the bill was not debated during any of its three readings in the *Bundestag* plenary, and instead was on the agenda of the parliament's interior affairs select committee (*Innenausschuss*) no fewer than eight times. A number of groups, including the UN High Commissioner for Refugees (UNHCR) and the Federal Administrative Court, as well as individuals, were consulted. The fact that the final version of the law, which came into force on 1 October 1965, was passed unanimously and with few amendments by the *Bundestag* may give some indication just how broad the consensus underpinning its formulation really was.

Even though the APVO had little credibility by virtue of its totalitarian provenance, Franz (1990) has pointed out that in some, admittedly subtle respects, the 1965 *Ausländergesetz* did not actually constitute much of an improvement for foreigners' residence. For instance, in Section 1, the new law stated that 'a residence permit may be issued if the presence of the foreigner does not compromise the interests of the Federal Republic of Germany'. In German legal terminology, this represents an important shift compared to the APVO, which made the issuing of a residence permit conditional on the worthiness of a foreigner. However, once this worthiness had been established, residence *had* to be permitted (the so-called *wird Bestimmung*). By contrast, under the 1965 *Ausländergesetz*, the foreigner's individual worthiness had no bearing whatsoever on the issue of a residence permit: the interests of the state were to be the sole determinant. Yet even if these did not rule out a foreigner's residence, a permit did not necessarily have to be issued (the so-called *darf Bestimmung*).

To complicate matters, neither the law nor its secondary legislation defined the 'interests of the Federal Republic of Germany' any further, and thus eschewed the 'hankering after definitional exactitude' Gordon Smith (1986: 209) has associated with German politics. Instead, the secondary legislation prescribed that residence permits should normally be issued for only one year in the first instance, and that any permit had to be denied if the non-national's residence was considered to be contrary to the 'Federal Republic's interests'. Effectively, the 1965 law made it considerably easier to justify legally both the denial and the revocation of a residence permit. Right from the start, the cards were therefore firmly stacked in the government's favour. It was this particular interpretation of the power relationship between the state and its non-national residents which was to be so central to policy debates in subsequent decades.

In light of this, it is perhaps surprising that the first commentaries of the new law were extremely benevolent, with its 'liberal character' being singled out for especial praise (Franz, 1992: 155). However, this period of grace was soon over, and opposition to the law's intentions and methods hardened from 1966 onwards. This opposition was to rumble on for almost a quarter of a century: it was not until 1990 that the eventual reform of this law, which is the subject of Chapter 3, could be completed.

The end of recruitment and its consequences, 1973–80

The first oil shock of 1973 signalled the end of the post-war economic boom years in Europe. In anticipation of the impact of higher oil prices on employment in Germany, the SPD–FDP coalition under Willy Brandt, which had also continued the CDU/CSU's guestworker policy upon assuming office in 1969, prohibited the further recruitment of labour on 23 November 1973. The so-called *Anwerbestopp*, which remained in force in 2002, changed the situation of those foreign workers remaining in West Germany overnight. Hitherto, workers who had returned to their countries of origin could entertain the possibility of further work in West Germany in the future. However, after the *Anwerbestopp* any guestworker who chose to leave would almost certainly leave for ever. With living standards in West Germany usually higher than in their countries of origin, many guestworkers unsurprisingly elected to stay.

They were in practice supported in their decision by industry, which had come to depend on the contribution of the foreign workforce to its output. With permanent contracts in their pockets, more and more of the remaining guestworkers began see their long-term perspectives in West Germany, and started to bring their wives and children to join them via family reunification (*Familiennachzug*) from 1973 and 1974 onwards. In addition, and partly as a result of this, the number of children born in Germany to non-national parents rose rapidly from 63,000 in 1970 to 108,000 in 1974, a figure representing a disproportionately high 17.3 per cent of all live births. The combination of these two factors had a substantial quantitative impact, as they more than compensated for any guestworkers departing after their contracts expired. Accordingly, the number of foreign residents in Germany increased from 4 million to 4.5 million between the end of recruitment in 1973 and 1980 (Table 2.1).

Table 2.1 Non-national population in West Germany, 1973–80

	1973	1974	1975	1976	1977	1978	1979	1980
Foreign population (m)	4.0	4.1	4.1	3.9	3.9	4.0	4.1	4.5
As % of total population	6.4	6.7	6.6	6.4	6.4	6.5	6.7	7.2
Foreign children born in Germany (000)	99	108	96	87	78	75	76	81
As % of all live births	15.6	17.3	16.0	14.4	13.4	13.0	13.0	13.0

Source: Collated from Beauftragte der Bundesregierung (2002: 423, 429).

Ironically, therefore, the *Anwerbestopp* played a central role in trans-forming the temporary guestworkers into a permanent immigrant minority (Bade, 1994: 46). In theory, longer residence also meant being able to apply for more secure levels of residence permit. But both federal and *Länder* governments were very slow to adapt to this. In the first instance, it was hoped and indeed expected that the remaining workers would return home as and when their contracts ran out. Bavaria and Baden-Württemberg even went so far as to segregate German and non-German children in its schools, on the basis that teaching the latter group in their mother tongues would foster a desire to return 'home' (Meier-Braun, 2002: 117).

At the same time, there was little enthusiasm for mass expulsions. Not only did foreign workers constitute a useful reserve pool of trained labour (Herbert, 2001), but mass forced repatriations were prohibited by the European Convention on Human Rights (ECHR) (Franz, 1992: 157) and would have severely damaged the standing of West Germany internationally. Instead, several unsuccessful attempts were made in the mid-1970s to prevent access to the labour market of foreign children and spouses, and these were replaced by general waiting periods for a work permit from 1979 onwards. In addition, a form of 'social engin-eering' was introduced, with the aim of preventing ghettoisation. Between 1975 and 1977, foreigners were banned from living in certain areas of large cities, as it was felt that a proportion of foreigners over 12 per cent of the population would be 'outside the limits of tolerance of the infrastructure and social peace' (Bade, 1994: 54). Such measures had little success and today most large industrial cities have a foreign share of inhabitants far above that limit, with Frankfurt's 30 per cent topping the chart.

The formulation of policy responses: the 1977 commission on *Ausländerpolitik*

Already by the mid-1970s, then, it had become increasingly obvious that a stable minority of non-Germans had formed. This development was entirely contrary to the intentions of the both the SPD-led federal government and the CDU/CSU-dominated *Länder* administrations. In a climate still dominated by labour market considerations, immigration not only meant a greater need for social infrastructure, but also increased pressure on what even then was considered to be a stagnating labour market. A new policy framework was required, and so a joint federation–*Länder* commission on the future direction of *Ausländerpolitik* was established on 4 August 1976, which reported back in April 1977. Its brief was to develop policies which reflected the fact that West Germany should not be considered 'a country of immigration'. The commission therefore marks the entry of this notorious maxim into policy positions, from which it was not to be dislodged for over twenty years. Its recommendations were as follows (Frey, 1982: 92–4):

- The *Anwerbestopp* should remain in force to prevent primary labour migration from non-EU countries

- Foreigners should be encouraged to return to their countries of origin

- The legal status of those families remaining should be increased and their integration into society promoted.

Overall, the commission's proposals mark the end of the dominance of labour market issues in *Ausländerpolitik* and the beginning of a broader policy framework. At the same time, their imprecision and the contradictory nature of the second and third goals was quite deliberate, as they represented a lowest-common-denominator approach to policy (cf. Katzenstein 1987: 218–19). Yet the three goals also had other, far-reaching implications for future policy content. In effect, they and their interpretation set the benchmark from which all future policy proposals had to depart. Moreover, given the cross-party consensus which underpinned them, they quickly came to be seen as the kind of 'optimal policy framework' from which divergence becomes difficult for normative reasons (Sturm, 1996: 120). They therefore constitute an absolutely critical source of the path dependency dynamics which were to dominate policy-making in subsequent decades. In fact, in the first ten years, any scope for political action was basically restricted to the question of which of the three goals should be given preference.

Initially, the SPD–FDP federal government focused on the third 'pillar', namely that of integration. It increased expenditure on social and integration projects almost six-fold (O'Brien, 1996: 55), and in 1979 adopted far-reaching and comprehensive recommendations for the integration of young foreigners agreed by the *Koordinierungskreis Ausländische Arbeitnehmer*, the tripartite consultation body at the Labour Ministry (BMA, 1986). More importantly, the federal government and *Bundesrat* in June 1978 agreed significant changes to the secondary legislation of the *Ausländergesetz*. This change had been prompted by a significant ruling from the Constitutional Court. Earlier that year, it had found that an Indian national, whose temporary residence permit had been routinely extended, but who had been refused an unlimited residence permit, enjoyed 'general trustworthiness' (*Vertrauensschutz*), which superseded the state's interests as a 'non-country of immigration' (for a full discussion, see Joppke, 1999: 73). *Inter alia*, the amendments gave foreigners the legal right to an unlimited residence permit after five years, in line with the general administrative practice which had developed hitherto.

The redefinition of citizenship? The 1977 Guidelines on Naturalisation

The government also made a first attempt to address the issue of naturalisation, in recognition of the fact that this would ultimately become an issue for those who stayed on in Germany permanently. In many ways this was the most sensitive of the areas tackled. For one thing, there was the problem of the GDR: as noted above, the very existence of East Germany made a redefinition of German citizenship away from the RuStAG difficult, as this would *ipso facto* dilute the pan-German definition taken over by West Germany. On the other hand, the presence of permanent non-ethnic German immigration made such an ethnocultural definition of citizenship totally unsuitable, as this would inherently and permanently exclude all immigrants from the German citizenry, with corresponding implications for democratic legitimacy and inclusion. The contradiction between Germany's exclusive citizenship definition and the reality of permanent immigration was thus one that needed to be resolved.

For this reason, the SPD-led government and CDU-led *Länder* on 15 December 1977 agreed a set of detailed guidelines on naturalisation

(*Einbürgerungsrichtlinien*), which, like the *Anwerbestopp*, remained in operation as of 2002. These fleshed out the otherwise surprisingly poorly defined requirements in the RuStAG for naturalisation (cf. Green, 2001b), by providing a comprehensive set of criteria upon fulfilment of which the applicant could be granted German citizenship, albeit without any certainty and subject to interpretation by the *Länder* as implementing agencies. The conditions included a recommended minimum of ten years' residence and, significantly for later debates, the requirement for the applicant to be released from his or her former citizenship. Helpfully, the guidelines also explained the overall standards to be employed by the bureaucracy in assessing applications. For instance, Section 2.2 states that 'naturalisation may only be considered if it is in the public interest … the personal and economic interests of the applicant cannot be the decisive factor'. In turn, the definition of the 'public interest' is confirmed in Section 2.3: 'the Federal Republic of Germany is not a country of immigration; it does not seek to increase the number of its citizens through naturalisation.'

But even if the naturalisation of a foreigner was seen to be in the public interest, the guidelines required the applicant to demonstrate a 'voluntary and lasting orientation towards Germany' (Section 3.1):

> The extent of the voluntary and lasting orientation towards Germany is to be determined by the applicant's entire attitude towards German culture. A lasting orientation or commitment to Germany is not evident if the applicant is active in émigré organisations … Naturalisation may not be granted solely for the economic benefit of the applicant, without evidence of an orientation towards Germany.

In other words, the guidelines resolved the contradiction between ethnocultural citizenship and non-ethnic immigration by emphasising the degree of cultural identification that would be expected of applicants. This was an important reorientation: any foreigner could, in theory at least, now become a German. However, the guidelines presupposed that non-nationals would voluntarily adopt this nebulous 'lasting orientation towards Germany', while simultaneously ruling out naturalisation before this orientation could be demonstrated by the applicant. More importantly, its emphasis on naturalisation as an exceptional act in Section 2.3 made it impossible for officials to be anything other than restrictive, as well as making a long and detailed scrutiny of individual applications inevitable. When combined with the rejection of dual citizenship and the very high levels of fees (three months' net income, up to ceiling of DM 5,000), the guidelines therefore simply did not make naturalisation an attractive option for foreigners, especially given the very high level of social and civil rights which were already available to them independently of nationality (Soysal, 1994). Accordingly, naturalisation rates during the 1980s (excluding ethnic Germans) remained negligibly low at around 0.3 per cent annually. In effect, the 1977 guidelines made West Germany's long-term resident non-nationals an offer of naturalisation they had no trouble refusing.

The inclusion of the principle of rejecting dual citizenship also merits explanation. In fact, this idea was relatively new to German citizenship law (the RuStAG made no mention of it for naturalisation), and stemmed legally from West Germany's accession (and subsequent strict adherence) to the 1963 Council of Europe Convention on the Reduction of Cases of Multiple Nationality. From 1969, it applied to the naturalisation of spouses of Germans, but it was only in the 1977 guidelines that this principle was extended to all naturalisations. In doing so, the government and the *Länder* drew on a famous Constitutional Court judgement of 1974, which considered multiple nationalities to be an 'evil' (*Übel*) (Joppke, 1999: 204–5). At the same time, there was never any suggestion that this principle was absolute: not only did the guidelines themselves list a range of cases in which dual citizenship would be tolerated in naturalisation, but ethnic Germans (*Aussiedler*) have always been permitted to retain their other nationality as a matter of course (Renner, 1999: 155).

Once the guidelines were in place, the dynamics of path dependency again kicked in. Henceforth, it proved to be practically impossible to revise the assumptions that the level of cultural integration for naturalisation should be high, that naturalisation should be an exception rather than the rule and that dual citizenship should be avoided if at all possible. Ironically, this need not have been so: the RuStAG was formulated so broadly that a swift, unbureaucratic naturalisation which accepted dual citizenship could easily have been compatible with its provisions. The controversy of later decades would thus have been nipped in the bud. Instead, the guidelines laid the foundations for two decades' worth of political disputes.

The Kühn Memorandum

Meanwhile, the Schmidt government demonstrated its new-found commitment to integration by appointing Heinz Kühn, the former SPD

Minister-President of North Rhine-Westphalia, as its first 'Federal Commissioner for the Integration of Foreign Workers and their Families' in
1978. In September 1979, he published the so-called 'Kühn Memorandum', in which he argued that the previous thrust of *Ausländerpolitik*
was no longer appropriate, given that 'an irreversible development has
set in, as a result of which the majority of foreigners are no longer
"guestworkers" but "immigrants", for whom a return to their countries
of origin is not feasible for a wide range of reasons' (Kühn, 1979).

The solution, according to Kühn, was to introduce a spread of policies
to recognise Germany's status as a country of immigration, including
a legal right to naturalisation for second-generation foreigners and local
voting rights for foreigners. Such far-reaching proposals sent political
shockwaves across the political spectrum: Kühn himself noted tartly
that 'not all of my cabinet colleagues considered the Memorandum to
be a gift from heaven' (Kühn, 1990: 10). Even so, given Kühn's status
as a senior SPD figure, the Schmidt government had little choice but
to take his proposals seriously: it had, after all, picked him for the job.
The fact that subsequent SPD initiatives on easier naturalisation and
later on local voting rights were first voiced in the Memorandum bears
evidence of his influence on his party's policy throughout the 1980s.

The timing of the Kühn Memorandum was unlucky: by 1980, popular
unease over the scale of immigration was growing. This sense of malaise
can be attributed to two factors: the increase in family reunification
following the *Anwerbestopp* and, more importantly, the eleven-fold
increase in asylum seekers between 1975 and 1980 to reach the hitherto
unprecedented level of 107,000 that year. The fact that asylum seekers
were at that time still allowed to work only served to stoke suspicion
that the applicants, most of whom came from Turkey, were simply
trying to obtain work permits via the 'back door' (Pirkl, 1982: 13). This
potent mix of issues produced a real fear of *Überfremdung*, of excessive
immigration which would make Germans strangers in their own country
(Thränhardt, 1988: 11–12). The publication in June 1981 of the so-called
'Heidelberg Manifesto', in which fifteen academics called for the maintenance of the cultural and linguistic purity of the German *Volk*,
provided an acceptable front to otherwise latent xenophobia (O'Brien,
1996: 78; see also Leuninger, 1983). The widespread suspicion of immigration among the population forced the federal government to
emphasise its restrictionist credentials, especially given the polarised
nature of the 1980 *Bundestag* election, in which Chancellor Schmidt
was challenged by the CSU's colourful and overtly conservative leader,

Franz Josef Strauss. Indeed, it was the SPD Minister-President of Hesse, Holger Börner, who in that year made the infamous electoral promise 'there'll be no more Turks coming to this state as long as I'm in charge' (quoted in Meier-Braun, 1995: 19; see also Meier-Braun, 2002: 53–6).

Here, then, was the first instance of 'issue spillover'. By 1980, as the Kühn Memorandum had acknowledged, many of the former guest-workers were permanently settled with their families; already, half the 4.5 million foreigners had lived in West Germany for ten or more years and their *de facto* integration was, at the very least, well under way. Their situation was thus vastly different from that of asylum seekers. Yet they were caught up in the public perception of excessive immigration that large numbers of asylum seekers helped to create. In turn, this impression determined the direction of policy for *all* foreigners, principally by the government's preference of restrictive immigration policies over the further consolidation of integration policies.

Nonetheless, these early years of *Ausländerpolitik* are characterised overall by a very high level of consensus (Katzenstein, 1987). All the interests and parties concerned considered labour migration as a temporary phenomenon which did not require substantial policy planning. Only when the ramifications of the *Anwerbestopp* gradually became clear by the mid-1970s was a shift in policy necessary, which was also accomplished in a spirit of cooperation. Accordingly, the recommendations of the 1977 commission, the changes to the administrative regulations in 1978 and the formulation of the Guidelines on Naturalisation all bear the mark both of cross-party consensus and cooperative federalism. However, the change of emphasis to restrictive policies in the early 1980s helped to hasten the breakdown in consensus that was to occur. The key event in this was the question of family reunification policy, which came to the forefront in late 1981.

Restricting secondary migration: the family reunification issue, 1980–82

Despite emerging victorious from the 1980 *Bundestag* election, the salience of *Ausländerpolitik* during the preceding years had left its mark on the ruling SPD–FDP coalition, especially as the opposition CDU/CSU continued to attack the government in its aftermath (Thränhardt, 1995a: 327–8). Polls showed that this policy area was fertile ground for the CDU/CSU's criticisms of government policy. In January 1981, the

Politbarometer poll showed that 66 per cent of respondents felt there were too many foreign workers in the country; by September 1982, shortly before the change of government, this had risen to 77 per cent (Forschungsgruppe Wahlen, 2000).

Faced with such entrenched public scepticism over immigration, the federal government became determined not to yield the initiative over restricting immigration to the CDU/CSU. At the same time, it had in early 1982 committed itself to the long-term integration of West Germany's foreign population (BMA, 1982). Thus the SPD–FDP coalition found itself attempting to reconcile the contradictory policy goals of restriction, repatriation and integration, as well as dealing with sustained criticism from the opposition. The fact that between 19 March 1980 and 14 July 1982 the federal government published no fewer than five sets of policy decisions in this area is an indication of the difficult political situation in which it found itself.

The result was that the profile of restriction and repatriation policies was further raised to exceed that of integrative policies. This took a number of forms. As well as tightening procedures for asylum seekers, in the form of revising the 1978 *Asylverfahrensgesetz*, a law to counteract illegal employment came into force on 1 January 1982. On 14 July 1982, the federal government also announced plans for a bill to promote voluntary repatriation. But most importantly, during 1981 it began to explore possibilities of restricting the migration of dependants to the largely male *Gastarbeiter* population. The problem was that such migration was not covered in the 1965 *Ausländergesetz*, and there was little coherent regulation of what had, since 1973, become a highly significant source of immigration. Now the government decided to act, both to limit the conditions under which spouses could immigrate (*Ehegattennachzug*) and, in particular, to lower from eighteen the age up to which children of foreigners could come to Germany (*Kindernachzug*).[6] In a keynote article in 1981, the Interior Minister, Gerhart Baum (FDP), expressed concern that foreigners who immigrated at age sixteen or seventeen often spoke little German and had received no relevant education to help them integrate into the German labour market. As he saw it, this would create 'a marginalised social group ... which has little chance of being integrated into [German] society in the course of time' (Baum, 1981: 8).

In particular, and foreshadowing the debates of later years, the proposals revolved around the question of whether to lower the age limit for *Kindernachzug* to sixteen or six, on the basis that the latter option ensured that children would receive their entire formal education in Germany. An age limit of six had been considered by Chancellor Helmut Schmidt and was indeed recommended by the Federal Minister for Labour Heinz Westphal (SPD) (Nave, 1983: 73). However, this caused outrage among the unions and churches, who countered such suggestions by emphasising the state's constitutional duty, enshrined in Article 6 of the Basic Law, to protect the rights of the family. In this, they were also supported by the FDP. The ensuing political impasse meant that no action was taken during the spring and summer of 1981.

But before this internal coalition conflict could be resolved, the matter was taken out of the federal government's hands. In September 1981, the CDU-ruled *Länder* of Baden-Württemberg, Schleswig-Holstein and West Berlin introduced unilateral restrictions on family reunification. The situation was considered acute in West Berlin, which in 1981 had the highest foreign proportion of all the *Länder* (12 per cent), numbering some 225,000 foreign residents. For its newly elected CDU government under Richard von Weizsäcker, family reunification was a problem which needed to be addressed as a matter of urgency. On 20 November 1981, the city's Interior Senator, Heinrich Lummer, reduced the age limit for young foreigners to join their parents from eighteen to sixteen. In addition, the regulations stipulated that both parents had to be ordinarily resident in West Germany. Foreigners reaching the age of eighteen would be required to return to their countries of origin, unless they had lived in Berlin for at least five years *and* were either in employment or training (details in Meier-Braun, 2002: 49–51). These regulations were modified slightly on 11 December 1981, but nonetheless represented the most radical attempt at restricting this form of immigration.

Legally, West Berlin, Baden-Württemberg and Schleswig-Holstein were well within their rights to act unilaterally: under Article 74 of the Basic Law, foreigners' residence falls under concurrent legislative jurisdiction of the federation and the *Länder*, leaving legislative competence with the *Länder* in the absence of a national regulation. But by breaking ranks with the other *Länder* and the federal government, the three 'renegades' forced Schmidt to act. However, time was not on the government's side: with the CDU-controlled *Bundesrat*, whose consent for such a law was required, pressing for a tough line, one observer estimated that a compromise would have taken months, if not years to achieve (Interview A). But with pressure mounting to find a solution, Schmidt asked the Interior Ministry to formulate a set of non-binding guidelines for all the *Länder* to follow. Given the perceived need to act quickly, such a set of guidelines were felt to be the best way to ensure common practice.

The urgency and political significance of these guidelines meant that they were approved by the federal cabinet on 2 December 1981, rather than taking the usual form of a recommendation to the existing horizontal coordinating mechanism, the Standing Conference of State Interior Ministers (*Innenministerkonferenz*, IMK) (Interviews A and B). They recommended that the *Länder* should exclude the following groups from family reunification:

- Anyone aged sixteen or above

- Children with only one parent living in Germany

- Dependants of foreigners living in Germany for the purposes of vocational training

- Spouses of foreigners who had come to Germany as children or had been born there, unless the foreigner had eight years' continuous residence, was at least eighteen years old and had been married for at least one year.

The guidelines represented a shrewd move by Schmidt: by taking the (relatively tough) West Berlin regulations as a model, the workings of cooperative federalism effectively left the *Länder* no option but to fall back in line, even though there was no formal legal requirement for them to do so. Indeed, most of the *Länder* did follow these recommendations, although there was some minor variation, towards both greater liberalism and tighter restrictions. Bremen continued to allow children up to the age of eighteen to immigrate, while Bavaria and Baden-Württemberg required spouses to be married for three years before they were granted residence. The two southern states' regulations were later struck down by the Constitutional Court in another important ruling (Joppke, 1999: 74–5).

Already the CDU/CSU-led *Länder* had threatened to go their own way and were prevented from doing so only by Chancellor Schmidt's swift compromise solution and by the norms of cooperative federalism which require the *Länder* to act together where possible. Significantly, the final outcome, by which the limit for *Kindernachzug* was lowered merely from eighteen to sixteen (as opposed to six), can in fact be considered incremental: the collective radical departure from established practice proved impossible to orchestrate. Nonetheless, the political dispute over family reunification represents a caesura in *Ausländerpolitik*, which effectively marks the end of cross-party consensus in this area. With the CDU/CSU rigorously emphasising the need to restrict immigration, the SPD–FDP government struggled to give equal attention to integration policy, in which it was supported by churches, welfare organisations and unions. It has often been overlooked that the government's policy statement on 2 December 1981 included not only the measures to reduce family reunification, but also announced a bill to give second-generation foreigners the right to naturalisation (Bundestagsdrucksache 9/1574), one of the Kühn Memorandum's chief ideas. Furthermore, in its policy decision of 3 February 1982, the government declared:

> The federal government is committed to the integration of permanently resident foreigners [in Germany] ... In order to improve their integration, the federal government is currently drafting a new *Ausländergesetz*, which will aim to place the residence of foreigners here on a more secure footing. (BMA, 1982: 18–19)

Ultimately, no progress was made towards this target. In February 1982, the naturalisation bill, which had been announced in December 1981, was rejected by the CDU/CSU-dominated *Bundesrat*. Moreover, the proposed new *Ausländergesetz* had yet to be introduced when, on 1 October 1982, the SPD–FDP coalition was replaced by a CDU/CSU–FDP government under Helmut Kohl.

Conclusion

By this time, the default position for future debate in each of the three areas on which this book is focusing had been set. In residence policy, the 1965 *Ausländergesetz*, in combination with the 1977 commission and the Guidelines on Naturalisation of the same year, had established the primacy of West Germany's interests as a non-immigration country. Moreover, by emphasising the exclusive nature of citizenship inherited from the 1913 RuStAG, the Guidelines on Naturalisation ruled out a simple solution to the legal marginalisation of long-term residents. Despite the party political controversy, the Guidelines on Family Reunification too represented an acceptable compromise between the federation and the *Länder*. The institutions of the semisovereign state were also clearly visible (cf. Katzenstein, 1987: Chapter 5). The fragmentation of state power between central and sub-national governments played a key role in bringing up the family reunification issue, while the norms of cooperative federalism helped ensure its resolution. The Constitutional Court's judgements proved important too, on the one hand helping to force policy-makers into making significant improvements to foreigners' rights, while also providing a legal justification for Germany's later principled opposition to dual citizenship (Joppke, 1999). Lastly, a cross-party consensus was clearly evident in the formulation of the *Ausländergesetz*, in the 1977 commission on *Ausländerpolitik* and in the Guidelines on Naturalisation.

But very soon, all three sets of parameters came to be challenged. During the 1980s and 1990s, the Right first attempted to change the position on family reunification and foreigners' residence, while the Left later sought to redefine the position on citizenship. But as the case studies in the following three chapters will show, the logic of the semisovereign state prevented either of these challenges from succeeding; instead, what policy change there was would be defined by incrementalism.

Notes

1 Fahrmeier (1997) maintains that this loss of citizenship upon emigration is not compatible with true *ius sanguinis*, and that as a result, the RuStAG constitutes a new departure in German citizenship. However, this arguably undervalues the fact that the principle of descent had already existed as the only formal method of ascription in German states' citizenship law for the best part of a century.

2 On the history of labour migration to West Germany generally, see Rist (1978), Edye (1987), Jamin (1999) and Herbert (2001).

3 Strictly speaking, it is not possible to separate guestworkers from other foreign workers in the official statistics, which show only those in tax-paying employment.

4 These original patterns of recruitment are reflected in the constitution by nationality of the foreign population in German towns. For instance, foreigners in Wolfsburg, the home of VW, are predominantly Italian, while in Cologne, the home of Ford, there is a large Turkish community.

5 From 1957 to 1961, the CDU/CSU had an absolute majority in the *Bundestag*. After the 1961 election, it formed a new coalition with the FDP, and in 1966 a grand coalition between CDU/CSU and SPD was established.

After the 1969 *Bundestag* election, the CDU/CSU went into opposition for the first time, as an SPD–FDP government under Willy Brandt took office.

6 The proposals applied only to secondary migration from countries outside the EU.

3

A policy reorientation? The Kohl government and the 1990 reform of the *Ausländergesetz*

When the CDU/CSU–FDP coalition under Helmut Kohl took office in late 1982, it was heralded, not least by itself, as the dawn of a dramatic era of change in policy, as the so-called *Wende*. It certainly seemed that substantive changes in *Ausländerpolitik* were likely, given both Kohl's focus on the issue in the previous two years and the importance he accorded it in his first parliamentary statement of government policy on 13 October 1982. In this, he made *Ausländerpolitik* one of the government's four priority areas for urgent action, a goal reiterated after his resounding victory at the 1983 *Bundestag* election.

However, the evidence of whether the Kohl government did actually bring about a *Wende* remains unclear. In his analysis of its deregulation policy, Webber (1992: 150) concludes that 'one could describe the policy changes which have occurred ... as a "halbe Wende", as a "semi-reorientation"'. A similar picture emerges in the area of *Ausländerpolitik* (Katzenstein, 1987). On the one hand, there was a clear toughening of rhetoric, and in contrast to the outgoing coalition, the emphasis on restricting immigration and on repatriation policies was initially increased at the expense of integration. As already noted in Chapter 2, this undoubtedly reflected popular concerns. Neither was there much appetite among voters for a more inclusive legal integration policy for foreigners: in September 1982's *Politbarometer*, 85 per cent of respondents agreed that the residence of foreigners should be limited, and 47 per cent replied that naturalisation should be made harder, not easier as the Schmidt government had proposed (Forschungsgruppe Wahlen, 2000). It is therefore hardly surprising that the proposals for a new *Ausländergesetz* and citizenship law were dropped outright.

On the other hand, the three goals which had been formulated in

1977 not only remained in place, but were actually confirmed by a second federation–*Länder* commission on *Ausländerpolitik* in 1983. Most existing integration policies and programmes were continued and some were even expanded (O'Brien, 1996: 87–9). In other areas, the new government's policy simply built on existing proposals by the outgoing SPD–FDP government. This continuity is exemplified by the fact that in 1984 the government made the significant concession that the naturalisation of foreigners was the long-term political goal, accepting that 'no state can in the long run accept that a significant part of its population remain outside the political community' (Bundestagsdrucksache 10/2071, quoted in Brubaker, 1992: 173).

At the same time, despite all the practical policy continuities, the formal positions of the three main parties continued on the trajectory of divergence which had emerged around the time of the asylum debate in 1980. Much of this policy difference was located at a more symbolic level, and dealt with issues such as whether West Germany was a country of immigration, rather than practical matters such as the problem of the already much higher levels of unemployment among foreign nationals. The principal agent in this divergence was the SPD, which used its freedom of opposition to pursue much more expansive policies, especially in the area of citizenship and legal integration. In doing so, it was also addressing the political challenge of the new left-wing force in West German politics, the Greens, to whom the SPD had lost votes in the 1983 federal election and whose proposals not only for free immigration but also for citizenship rights detached from nationality far exceeded those of the other parties (see Murray, 1994). By contrast, the CDU/CSU found that the realities of government, in combination with the Constitutional Court's judgements outlined in Chapter 2, simply precluded highly restrictive policy solutions.

Meanwhile, the CDU/CSU–FDP coalition also found itself increasingly at odds with itself. Hardliners such as the new Interior Minister, Friedrich Zimmermann (CSU), were opposed by most of the CDU's influential social-catholic wing under Labour Minister Norbert Blüm and the party's general secretary Heiner Geißler (O'Brien, 1996: 89–96). They were invariably joined by the liberal FDP, which in turn made a point of supporting the new Commissioner for Foreigners Affairs, Liselotte Funcke, herself also an FDP member. Broadly speaking, this cleavage within the CDU has remained ever since, and Chapter 4 will highlight its significance for the debate over citizenship policy in the 1990s.

Overall, Katzenstein's conclusion that the CDU/CSU-led government's policy in practice 'is distinguishable from that of its SPD
predecessor only in matters of detail' (Katzenstein, 1987: 228) seems
fair. Yet this holistic sense of continuity obscures the fact that, in
Ausländerpolitik at least, the 1980s saw several attempts, from both sides
of the political spectrum, to redefine the agenda and impose more
sweeping changes. The key point for this book is that the absence of
consensus brought the semisovereign institutional structures of the West
German state into play, which in turn meant that any far-reaching
proposals in either direction stood little chance of success. This is
particularly borne out in the drawn-out debate over the reform of the
1965 *Ausländergesetz*. This became a central issue of domestic politics
in the late 1980s and will be the subject of detailed consideration in the
latter part of this chapter. But first, some of the other issues to feature
in this decade will be discussed briefly.

Ausländerpolitik in the 1980s: between repatriation and integration

The 1983 commission on Ausländerpolitik

The extent to which the parties' formal conceptions of *Ausländerpolitik*
had diverged was highlighted in the second joint federation–*Länder*
commission on *Ausländerpolitik*, which was established on 13 October
1982, with a brief to report back in time for the upcoming *Bundestag*
election in March 1983. Its deliberations, which were in part conducted
at ministerial level, attempted to address all relevant issues in an effort
to establish common ground for future action, and its report was
presented on 24 February 1983. Overall, the commission laboured to
establish any areas of consensus beyond confirming the three broad
goals which had already been established by the first commission of
1977. In particular, it proved impossible to find common ground on
the sensitive issue of the immigration of minor dependants (*Kindernachzug*), in which Interior Minister Zimmermann advocated an age
limit of six. The divergence in positions transcended party political and
territorial interests: even the CDU/CSU-led federal ministries represented were unable to agree (Haberland, 1983). In consequence, this
particular policy goal was dropped in 1984 in a statement of the
government's position on *Ausländerpolitik* (Bundestagsdrucksache
10/2071).

Three things are particularly noteworthy about the 1983 commission. First, with such a lack of agreement, it was never going to be able to address the inherently contradictory nature of the 1977 goals. These consequently remained valid, and thereby continued to have a path defining impact. Instead, it devoted its attention to more technical aspects of managing these three goals (Haberland, 1983). Thus the commission agreed that

- The discretionary criteria of the 1965 *Ausländergesetz* for the granting of an unlimited residence permit should be replaced by concrete entitlements (*Rechtsansprüche*)

- Family reunification should be regulated by law instead of the guidelines of 1981

- Naturalisation should be made easier for second-generation foreigners

- A new form of residence permit should be introduced for students and other short-term visitors, which would by definition preclude permanent residence

- Specific reasons for refusing a residence permit should be included in the law.

Second, the commission confirmed both the path dependency dynamics and the lowest-common-denominator approach of its 1977 predecessor: indeed, many of its conclusions merely formalised the existing administrative practice following the 1978 amendments to the secondary legislation of the *Ausländergesetz*; in turn, these conclusions were to form the basis of the law's reform in 1990. The third point is the significance of the fact that the proposal to reduce the scope for *Kindernachzug*, which had the expressed blessing of Interior Minister Zimmermann, had eventually to be dropped. This underlines precisely the limits of executive autonomy in policy-making Katzenstein identified, which were to become more clearly visible in the late 1980s, when the Interior Ministry's first concrete proposals for a new *Ausländergesetz* were leaked.

Voluntary repatriation, citizenship and asylum

Notwithstanding the broad overall continuity between the Schmidt and Kohl governments, there was still a palpable change of policy emphasis to back up the toughened rhetoric. Already in September 1982, shortly before the change of government, Kohl had called for a reduction in the number of foreigners in West Germany by 1 million. In the absence of either the legal or political option of instituting large-scale expulsions, this promise was to be delivered by a new law on voluntary repatriation, which provided financial incentives for former guestworkers and their families to return to their countries of origin. From 1 December 1983, the law offered foreigners the value of their contributions to the state pension fund plus a premium of DM 10,500 if they left West Germany (details in O'Brien, 1996: 81–3). These measures had only a limited effect, as they were offset by new immigration (for instance, in the form of asylum seekers) and the continued high birth rate among foreigners. The overall number of foreigners in West Germany thus failed to drop significantly between 1982 and 1984. This in turn raised the suspicion that the law only encouraged those foreigners who were already planning to leave to bring forward their departure, and the government opted not to renew the legislation when it expired on 31 December 1984. As the 1980s progressed, so the number of foreigners in West Germany began to rise again and by 1988 stood at just below its 1983 level; by 1989, it had exceeded it to stand at 4.8 million, or 7.7 per cent of the population (Table 3.1).

The failure of these repatriation policies inevitably brought the third goal of the 1977 commission, the promotion of integration, back onto the agenda. Although the residence periods of the former guestworkers and their families were increasing steadily, their social and legal status was advancing only marginally. As Günter Walraff's 1985 polemic *Ganz Unten* showed, life for foreigners was frequently defined by pervasive discrimination and marginalisation (Walraff, 1985). Legally too, the change in the *Ausländergesetz*'s secondary legislation in 1978 made little discernible difference: despite that fact that in 1988 almost 60 per cent of foreigners had residence periods in West Germany of ten years or longer, the majority were still in possession of merely a temporary residence status, providing them with little security from expulsion in the case of unemployment or sickness. Indeed, this blatant gap between residence period and status, which has persisted into the new millennium (cf. Appendix), raises questions to what extent the blame lies with the authorities, by not actively promoting the possibility of permanent residence (Bischoff and Teubner, 1992: 73).

German citizenship, too, remained an exceptional prize: as Table 3.1 shows, the proportion of the foreign population naturalised annually

Table 3.1 Immigration and the non-national population in West Germany, 1981–90

	1981	1982	1983	1984	1985	1986	1987	1988	1989	1990
Foreign population (m)	4.6	4.7	4.5	4.4	4.4	4.5	4.2	4.5	4.8	5.3
As % of total population	7.5	7.6	7.4	7.1	7.2	7.4	6.9	7.3	7.7	8.4
Foreign children born in Germany, as % of all live births	12.8	11.8	10.4	9.4	9.2	9.4	10.5	10.9	11.7	11.9
Naturalisation rate (%)	0.3	0.3	0.3	0.3	0.3	0.3	0.3	0.4	0.4	0.4
New asylum applications (000)	49	37	20	35	79	100	57	103	121	193
Ethnic German immigrants (000)	69	48	38	36	39	43	79	203	377	397

Sources: Collated from Green, 2001a; Beauftragte der Bundesregierung (2002); Bundesverwaltungsamt.

(the naturalisation rate) remained negligible for all intents and purposes during the 1980s. Apart from its 1984 admission that naturalisation was a long-term policy goal, citizenship never really featured prominently on the Kohl government's radar between 1982 and 1990. For one thing, the continuing division of Germany continued to preclude any substantive redefinition of citizenship away from its existing, pre-1945 form. No less important in practical terms was the fact that the government was keen to promote a more positive perception of German values, as exemplified by the so-called *Historikerstreit* (historians' dispute) in the mid-1980s over the interpretation of Germany's Nazi past (O'Brien, 1996: 75). In terms of *Ausländerpolitik*, this ruled out a more inclusive naturalisation policy, which might have entailed persons who were not fully committed to the maintenance of Germany's cultural identity from gaining legal parity through citizenship. For many government supporters, a liberal citizenship law smacked of what they considered to be the Greens' pernicious multicultural agenda.

In parallel to this, the policy agenda in the 1980s continued to be influenced by fears over the numbers seeking political asylum and the perception that this mechanism was being misused for economic reasons (Thränhardt, 1995a). Although the number of applications had dropped from its provisional peak in 1980 to just 20,000 in 1983, it once again exceeded 100,000 by 1986. In 1987, it also emerged that the GDR was permitting asylum seekers to fly to East Berlin, from where they were literally dumped at the border to West Berlin to apply for asylum there. In reply, the Kohl government passed two further revisions of the Asylum Procedural Law (*Asylverfahrensgesetz*) in 1987 and 1988, as well as prevailing on the GDR to close this loophole. However, this had little overall impact: in 1988, the number of asylum seekers again broke the politically sensitive 100,000 barrier (see Table 3.1). As a result, some voices in the CDU/CSU began to suggest that the constitutionally enshrined right to asylum be amended in order to curtail this immigration flow, although this proposal did not gather momentum until after unification.

Meanwhile, Chancellor Kohl paid the political price for failing to fulfil his 1982 promise to reduce the number of foreigners in West Germany. Fears over the level of immigration and especially asylum were increasing: in July 1989, 86 per cent of respondents in the *Politbarometer* opinion poll thought there were too many asylum seekers. Indeed, in 1989, immigration topped the *Politbarometer*'s survey of the nation's most pressing political problems (Forschungsgruppe Wahlen, 2000). It was thus almost inevitable that this unease should translate into electoral success for the extreme Right (Chapin, 1997: 57–9, 78–85). Already the new force on the Right, the *Republikaner*, led by the former SS-officer and CSU politician Franz Schönhuber, had scored a respectable 3 per cent at the 1986 Bavarian *Land* election, quite enough to make the incumbent CSU sit up and take note. Then, at the Berlin Senate election on 29 January 1989, the *Republikaner* became the first extremist party since the NPD in 1968 to achieve representation at *Land* level, taking 7.5 per cent of the vote. In turn, the NPD itself scored 6.6 per cent local elections in Frankfurt on 12 March 1989. Worse was to come at the European Parliament (EP) elections on 18 June 1989, when the *Republikaner* scored 7.1 per cent of the vote nationally, and an astonishing 14.6 per cent in Bavaria.

The debate over local voting rights

In addition to asylum, the issue of local voting rights for foreigners also emerged as a source of 'issue spillover' in the late 1980s, and came to dominate all discussions about the integration of foreigners. In his Memorandum of 1979, Heinz Kühn had proposed that foreigners be granted such rights in order to promote their integration by encouraging their political participation at local level. This idea was enthusiastically supported by both foreigners' groups and the German Trade Union Federation (*Deutscher Gewerkschaftsbund*, DGB), and had the strong political backing of the SPD and the Greens. The CDU/CSU-led federal government, by contrast, totally rejected the idea, arguing that such a move would effectively remove one of the prime incentives for naturalisation, which had, after all, been identified as the overall political aim in 1984. Brubaker echoes this reservation:

> This concern with partial civic conclusion outside of formal citizenship has distracted attention from the question of formal citizenship status and delayed full recognition of the anomalous formal citizenship status of Germany's increasingly settled immigrants. (Brubaker, 1992: 178)

The issue was therefore a poor choice with which to champion the interests of foreigners, as it not only detracted from the more pressing issues of residence and naturalisation, but also received little sympathy from the public. It finally came to a head in 1989, when the SPD-led states of Hamburg and Schleswig-Holstein introduced laws to enfranchise foreigners at local elections. The CDU/CSU, together with the state of Bavaria, successfully sought closure of the issue before the Constitutional Court, which on 31 October 1990 ruled that, under Article 20 of the Basic Law, the right to vote was limited to the 'German people', thereby excluding foreigners (see Joppke, 1999: 194–9 for a full discussion of this matter). This judgement effectively closed off the avenue of granting suffrage independently of citizenship, although Article 8 of the 1992 TEU later granted local and European voting rights to all EU citizens. For Joppke (1999: 195), this issue constituted a 'foundational debate over the meaning of membership and citizenship in the nation-state'. But it also once again graphically illustrated the formidable ability of the Constitutional Court to limit the range of options available to policy-makers.

Bringing the *Ausländergesetz* back into play, 1982–87

Of much greater importance for the development of *Ausländerpolitik* overall was the protracted debate over the reform of the 1965 *Ausländergesetz*, and the associated regulation of family reunification, residence and naturalisation. As Chapter 2 has noted, opposition to the law had begun to form very soon after its enactment, and this was led by the

unions and churches, together with their associated welfare organisations. However, because the law fell under the remit of the Interior
Ministry, such interests, who were instead networked in with the Labour
Ministry (Katzenstein, 1987), were able to make little headway with
their agenda. By the time the Schmidt government began to tackle a
reform of the law, serious differences of opinion had thus opened up
between the federal government and the relevant actors of centralised
society. These differences were only accentuated after the SPD left government in 1982. The remainder of this chapter will be dedicated to an
examination of how and why the reform did ultimately materialise, and
how Germany's semisovereign structures can help explain its outcome.

As part of the changeover of government, the FDP lost control of the
Interior Ministry, which it had held since 1969. Instead, this was allocated
to the Bavarian CSU, for whom *Ausländerpolitik* and law-and-order issues
more generally were of defining importance. The then CSU leader, Franz
Josef Strauss, had repeatedly stated that there should be no democratically
legitimated party to the right of the CSU (quoted in Mintzel, 1992: 264).
The choice of the Interior Ministry as its most senior cabinet post, and
the appointment of Friedrich Zimmermann, a close confidant of Strauss,
as Minister thus reflected the potential the CSU saw in *Ausländerpolitik*
for pre-empting protest votes for extreme right-wing parties. As noted,
as well as shelving the SPD's plans for a new *Ausländergesetz*, Zimmermann turned his attention to more restrictive policies, including the
reduction of the maximum age for *Kindernachzug* and the introduction
of the voluntary repatriation programme for resident foreigners. These
initiatives were spiced up with some aggressive rhetoric. For instance,
in summer 1983 he summarised the aims of a future reform of the 1965
Ausländergesetz by emphasising only the restrictive elements of the 1983
commission's final report (see above):

> The establishment of concrete reasons for refusing a residence permit; the
> creation of a temporally limited residence permit, which from the outset
> precludes a later permanent residence; the extension of the requirement
> for a residence permit to foreigners under 16 years of age. (*Frankfurter
> Rundschau*, 19 July 1983, quoted in Çelik, 1995)

In fact, the Interior Ministry had already produced a second new draft
for the reform of the *Ausländergesetz* within one year of this statement.
Yet despite the nominally high priority given to *Ausländerpolitik* by
Chancellor Kohl after the 1983 election, the new draft was not taken up
by Zimmermann, who preferred to focus his efforts on the government's

policy of encouraging voluntary repatriation and reducing the maximum age for *Kindernachzug* (Interview A). Following the failure of these policies, other issues spilled over onto the Interior Ministry's agenda: apart from asylum, the government was very concerned that the free movement of labour might be extended to Turkey by virtue of its 1963 Association Agreement with the EU, thereby raising fears of a whole new phase of Turkish immigration. It was not until late 1986 that this latter issue could be resolved in Germany's favour (see Herbert, 2001: 257–9).

By 1987, though, it had become clear that a reform of the *Ausländergesetz* could not be delayed much longer. With the failure of voluntary repatriation policies, and the restriction of family reunification beyond the 1981 compromise also off the table, the question of addressing the continuing poor legal situation of foreigners inevitably returned to the political agenda. Here, the need for action was greater than ever. There was mounting criticism of the *Ausländergesetz*'s broad discretionary regulations, which commentators felt to be incompatible with the rule of law (the principle of the *Rechtsstaat*) (e.g. Zuleeg, 1984). The CDU/CSU–FDP government's formal intention to reform the 1965 *Ausländergesetz* was thus announced on 18 March 1987 by Chancellor Kohl in his governmental programme following the federal election that January; indeed, Interior Minister Zimmermann initially aimed to enact such a reform by the end of that year (*Frankfurter Allgemeine Zeitung*, 3 October 1987).

The Interior Ministry and the CSU attempt to set the agenda, 1987–89

This announcement set off a flurry of activity by the Commissioner for Foreigners' Affairs, Liselotte Funcke, as well as the interest groups active in this area, who first issued and then coordinated their ideas on the shape of the new law (Barwig, 1988; Beauftragte der Bundesregierung, 1988). After five years of fighting a rearguard action against the CSU's and Interior Minister Zimmermann's proposals for restriction, they at last saw the intended reform as an opportunity to move forward again and liberalise what they considered to be the excessively restrictive emphasis of the 1965 law. But as was to become abundantly clear during 1988, the Interior Ministry's political leadership had somewhat different priorities. Indeed, the controversy over the Interior Ministry's draft proposals of 1988 laid bare not only the divisions between government and opposition, but also underlined the differences of opinion *within* the governing coalition.

In April 1988, a substantial, 133-page-long internal draft for the reform of the *Ausländergesetz* (BMI, 1988), dated 1 February 1988, was leaked to the *Arbeiterwohlfahrt* social welfare organisation. The draft was passed on to the magazine *Der Spiegel* which reported on it during April of that year (*Der Spiegel*, 4 April and 18 April 1988). Once the full text had been examined, it sent shockwaves not only through interest groups, but also the political parties. The draft proposed replacing the existing law with not one, but two new laws. The first, the Foreigners' Integration Law (*Ausländerintegrationsgesetz*), was aimed at raising the residential status of existing immigrants, by granting them, subject to further conditions, unlimited residence permits (even in the case of unemployment) and permitting family reunification, including the immigration of children up to the age of sixteen. However, despite the accompanying commentary's stated aim of creating conditions of legal certainty (*Rechtssicherheit*), there was to be no general legal right to the law's provisions (*Rechtsanspruch*), only 'as a rule' (*Regelanspruch*), which shifted the burden of proof for denial onto the authorities, but no more. Moreover, the law made no reference to any new naturalisation procedures.

By contrast, the second law, provisionally entitled Foreigners' Entry Law (*Ausländeraufnahmegesetz*), which was to work in tandem with the first law, contained a comprehensive catalogue of measures designed to prevent any new immigration to West Germany. As with the Foreigners' Integration Law, the draft's stated aim of creating *Rechtssicherheit* was contradicted by the continued wide range of discretion accorded to the authorities. Although, in contrast to the 1965 *Ausländergesetz*, the Foreigners' Entry Law was specifically to take account of the interests of an immigrant (Section 4), the Federal Republic's interests were to retain primacy in all decisions on whether a residence permit should be issued in the first instance (Sections 7 and 8). In particular, Section 11 provided for an unlimited residence permit to be issued only in individually justifiable cases (*begründeten Einzelfällen*): the accompanying commentary notes bluntly that 'the regularisation of residence is no longer to be the rule, but rather the exception' (BMI, 1988: 31).

Crucially, the proposal for the Foreigners' Entry Law also stipulated that foreigners were not to receive limited residence permits indefinitely: after eight years, the authorities would have to decide once and for all whether to grant an unlimited residence permit or whether the foreigner's residence in West Germany should be terminated. Yet the renewal of residence permits up to this limit was to be dependent on the foreigner's willingness to return to his or her country of origin. Thus, in practice, a foreigner would be allowed to remain in the country only if he or she could show that they were in reality planning to leave (Prantl, 1994: 70).

In the contentious area of family reunification, a right to *Kindernachzug* was to exist only until the age of six, although the authorities could permit the immigration of children up to the age of sixteen, but with no legal compulsion. Under Section 37 of the Foreigners' Entry Law, non-nationals could even be expelled for disparagement of the Federal Republic or its constitutional institutions. Finally, the administrative fees for obtaining a residence permit were to be increased to a basic fee of DM 150 plus DM 7.50 per month of the residence period applied for, up to a discouraging maximum of DM 1,000 for an unlimited residence permit.

The commentary which accompanied the draft legislation enlarged candidly on the rationale behind the two laws. According to this, their aim was 'to safeguard [Germany's] national characteristics' (BMI, 1988: 24) by preventing further immigration which, if allowed to continue unchecked, would lead to the

> abandonment of societal homogeneity, which is primarily determined by membership of the German nation. Germany's common history, heritage, language and culture would lose their unifying and defining nature. The Federal Republic would develop little by little into a multinational and multicultural community, which would over time be weighed down by the resulting problems with its minorities. (BMI, 1988: 23)

This general goal of societal homogeneity had, so the draft said, important policy implications: 'the regulation of foreigners' legislation must therefore take place under the assumption that, over time, the Federal Republic of Germany will be faced with the problem of repelling an unmanageable level of immigration by foreigners' (BMI, 1988: 24).

Once in the public domain, this proposal proved to be political dynamite, and effectively delayed the reform of the *Ausländergesetz* by over eighteen months. It was roundly rejected by the churches, the unions, by the SPD and the Greens, by the FDP and, most importantly, by sections of the CDU (Bade, 1994: 62). The controversy was increased by the fact that the SPD, FDP and the social-catholic wing of the CDU, the *Christlich-Demokratische Arbeitnehmerschaft* (CDA), had all published their own proposals for the new law in February of that year, prior to the draft's emergence (Barwig, 1988). All of these saw the reform of the *Ausländergesetz* as an opportunity for advancing legal integration, rather than placing the emphasis on restrictive, defensive measures as the Foreigners' Entry Law did. Indeed, the CDA proposed not only the issue of a 'residence entitlement' (the most secure form of residence status) after five years and the possibility of *Kindernachzug* up to the age of eighteen, but also envisaged a legal entitlement to naturalisation under certain circumstances (CDA, 1988).

The criticism of the Interior Ministry's proposals was almost universal. The *Arbeiterwohlfahrt*'s chief official for foreigners' affairs, Eberhard de Haan, argued that, far from improving the situation of foreigners in Germany, the two laws in fact made their lives less certain (de Haan, 1988). Similarly, the *Diakonisches Werk*, the Protestant Church's welfare organisation, criticised that the maintenance of broad administrative discretion in the draft laws transformed the permission of residence to a foreigner into an act of mercy by the authorities (*behördlicher Gnadeakt*) (Diakonisches Werk, 1989).

Nor did the draft find many political friends. While the SPD and Greens might have been expected to reject the Interior Ministry's proposals, the FDP, too, was resolutely opposed, with its parliamentary spokesman on internal affairs, Burkhard Hirsch, describing the proposals as 'extraordinarily narrow-minded' (*Der Spiegel*, 18 April 1988). The chorus of disapproval also reached well into the CDU/CSU parliamentary party. The CDU's general secretary, Heiner Geißler, condemned the draft's persistent denial that Germany was a country of immigration. The CDU/CSU's own influential interior affairs spokesman, Johannes Gerster, criticised the draft's contents during an emergency debate in the *Bundestag* (Deutscher Bundestag Plenarprotokoll 11/88). The controversy at parliamentary level might have dragged on for much longer, had it not been for the fact that the proposals were debated during the last plenary before that year's summer recess. Interior Minister Zimmermann reacted by first denying the draft's existence and then by distancing himself from it, arguing (rather implausibly) that it only represented a so-called *Referentenentwurf*, or internal draft, and thus had not been adopted by the Ministry's political leadership. Nonetheless, this did not prevent discussions between the Interior and Justice Ministries over a possible new law on its basis in late 1988 (*Der Spiegel*, 28 November 1988).

The emergence of these two draft laws in 1988 represents a caesura in the debate over the content of the new *Ausländergesetz*. Hitherto, Zimmermann's ideas and priorities had been the subject of speculation, but with no concrete proposals available, societal groups remained in the dark over what his plans were in detail. However, the Interior Ministry's paper changed all this. Prantl (1994: 69) notes that the eighty-two sections of the Entry Law, compared to the seventeen sections of the Integration Law, gave some indication as to which of the two was seen as the more important by the Interior Ministry. Zimmermann, and by extension the CSU leadership, whose confidence he enjoyed, had effectively revealed their hand – and found that no-one was willing to play. The resulting isolation of Zimmermann and the proposals prepared for him by the Interior Ministry had far-reaching consequences both for the eventual content of the new law and for its formulation. First, Zimmermann's attempt to impose his ideas had failed because the state's semisovereignty required the support of other institutions, notably of the governing political parties, for the proposals to have any chance of success. A compromise thus became necessary. However, the perceived 'overkill' of the Interior Ministry's ideas had reduced its credibility to broker such a deal. Second, there was little political agreement within the government over whether the new law should consist of a radical tightening of immigration and residence law, or whether the emphasis should be on improving conditions for foreigners. These differences in opinion split the CDU/CSU itself, frustrating the formation of the 'minimum-winning coalition' necessary to pass the reform and instead promoting a temporary non-decision. Third, the adverse publicity created by the drafts severely damaged the standing of Interior Minister Friedrich Zimmermann and signalled the beginning of the end of his tenure in this position.

The road to reform, 1989–90

The evident political unacceptability of the Interior Ministry's drafts was illustrated beyond doubt by the negotiations conducted between the Interior and Justice Ministries in late 1988.[1] Held at the highest administrative level, they were of a political as well as technical nature, with the participants, *Staatssekretäre* Neusel and Kinkel, searching for common ground for a political solution. Significantly, none was found, with most of the discussions being referred up to the respective ministers for a decision (*Der Spiegel*, 28 November 1988).

Evidently, the impasse created by the two draft laws could not be resolved as long as Zimmermann remained Interior Minister. In addition to his policy positions, his handling of the drafts, first denying their existence and then playing down their significance, had undermined his authority in the cabinet. In effect, Zimmermann had become a lame duck. The final blow came in early April 1989, when he was demoted to Transport Minister in Chancellor Kohl's ministerial reshuffle. The entry of the new CSU leader Theo Waigel into the cabinet as Finance Minister also signalled the end of Zimmermann's position as senior CSU minister.

His successor at the Interior Ministry was Wolfgang Schäuble, a rising star in the CDU. During his time as Minister of State at the Federal Chancellery from 1984 to 1989, Schäuble had gained a reputation as an effective manager, and he brought a new pragmatic approach to the business of reforming the *Ausländergesetz*. Above all, he realised that an eventual new draft, in order for it to have any chance of becoming law, would require a broader consensual base, at the very least within the ruling coalition (Interview B).

His pragmatism was also influenced by two other exogenous factors. First, there were fears of a resurgence of extreme right-wing parties in the late 1980s: as noted above, the *Republikaner* party had scored some spectacular successes in 1989, especially by scoring 14.6 per cent in Bavaria in the European election of that year. With a *Land* election due in Bavaria in September 1990, a sense of urgency developed in the federal coalition generally but especially within the CSU. As a result, the reform of the *Ausländergesetz* was not only to be completed before the series of elections due in 1990, but it was to be handled in such a way as not to give ammunition to the extreme right-wing. The political prerequisites for a compromise solution, especially for the CSU, were thus falling into place.

But pressure to act also came from a second quarter. Throughout the 1980s, the CDU/CSU, either alone or in coalition with the FDP, had enjoyed a comfortable majority of states' votes in the *Bundesrat*. However, towards the end of the 1980s, this majority began to crumble. Following the loss of Schleswig-Holstein to the SPD in May 1988, the number of *Länder* in the CDU/CSU bloc was reduced to five (excluding West Berlin). The next key state election was scheduled for 13 May 1990, when the incumbent CDU/CSU–FDP government in Lower Saxony under Ernst Albrecht would be challenged by an up-and-coming SPD politician, Gerhard Schröder. If Albrecht lost the election, the CDU/CSU would lose its majority in the *Bundesrat* and thus be dependent on the SPD for compromise (Table 3.2). This was to be avoided at all costs.

Table 3.2 The erosion of the CDU/CSU majority in the *Bundesrat*, 1988–90

	Distribution of votes in the *Bundesrat* after *Land* elections which produced a change of government		
	Hesse 5 April 1987 (SPD–Green to CDU–FDP)	Schleswig-Holstein 8 May 1988 (CDU–FDP to SPD)	Lower Saxony 13 May 1990 (CDU–FDP to SPD–Greens)
A-*Länder* votes	14	18	23
B-*Länder* votes	27	23	18

Note: 'A-*Länder*' are SPD-led *Länder*, 'B-*Länder*' are CDU/CSU-led *Länder*. West Berlin, where an SPD–Green government replaced the CDU–FDP government in January 1989, also had four delegates, but without voting rights: they are not included in the above figures.
Source: Based on information contained in Andersen and Woyke (1997: 650–1).

In effect, therefore, the delay brought about by the controversy over the Interior Ministry's drafts placed the government in a potentially unfavourable political situation, which was to influence both the way in which the final version of the new *Ausländergesetz* was passed, as well as its content.

The new Ausländergesetz *takes shape*

Already on 14 February 1989, the interior spokesmen of the coalition's three parliamentary parties (*Fraktionen*) had been charged by Wolfgang Schäuble, who was then still at the Federal Chancellery, with the task of formulating the political parameters (*Eckwerte*) for the reform of the *Ausländergesetz*. Their negotiations lasted two months, and the resulting blueprint for the new law, while representing a significant departure from the 1988 proposals, was substantially based on the conclusions of the 1983 commission. Thus, in addition to enshrining current administrative practice on residence permits and family re-unification in law, the *Eckwerte* paper also supplemented the provisions of the 1977 Guidelines on Naturalisation by introducing a process of 'simplified naturalisation' (*erleichterte Einbürgerung*) for young (i.e. usually second-generation) foreigners aged between sixteen and twenty-one.

Because its content largely reflected the recommendations of the 1983 commission, the paper contained few new policy initiatives. Yet politically, it was a welcome relief from the restrictive emphasis of the 1988 drafts. Crucially, by involving all the coalition partners in the negotiations, the paper created the foundations of a parliamentary majority which the Ministry's dual proposals of 1988 simply did not enjoy. The paper even received a positive reception from the SPD. Liselotte Funcke, the Commissioner for Foreigners' Affairs, was more guarded; she was criticical that the formal criteria for family reunification and the granting of an unlimited residence permit had been extended to include adequate living space, a requirement which many non-nationals found difficult to fulfil (Beauftragte der Bundesregierung, 1989a).

Notwithstanding her reservations, the paper did generate broad goodwill. It also raised expectations that a cross-party solution to include the SPD could be found, in the hope of sending a positive signal to the foreign population and a synchronous rejection to the extreme right-wing. Such hopes were soon to be dashed: already, Klaus Barwig, writing earlier in mid-1989, had warned almost prophetically:

> Both formally and in terms of content, it seems that excessive optimism with regard to a cross-party consensus in *Ausländerpolitik* is premature ...
> In spite of the momentum, which has rather surprisingly been injected into the policy discussion and in spite of the agreement over the options for improvement, the controversy over the core issues remains substantial. (Barwig, 1989: 125)

With the Interior Ministry working on the new bill based on this paper during the summer of 1989, Interior Minister Schäuble was able to present what was in effect the fourth version of the new law to the public on 29 September 1989. This now took the form of one law instead of the two pieces of legislation which had been proposed in 1988. As a result of codifying what had over time become accepted administrative practice and of replacing executive discretion with concrete legal rights and entitlements, the draft was both long (over 100 sections) and extremely complex.

The response from commentators was inconclusive. Kay Hailbronner, a leading academic lawyer, gave it a qualified endorsement, concluding that, despite room for improvement, the proposals addressed the main regulatory issues in a satisfactory way (Hailbronner, 1990). Similarly, Eckart Schiffer, the head of the Interior Ministry's division (*Abteilung*) on foreigners, which had drafted the new law, presented it as a sensibly crafted consensus between all political positions, which would provide foreigners living in West Germany with significant improvements (Schiffer, 1990).

On the other hand, the response to the draft from societal interest groups was muted. The *Arbeiterwohlfahrt* saw considerable similarities to the 1988 proposals (AWO, 1989), while the unions, represented by the DGB, noted that 'the draft represents a worsening of the existing legislation in many areas' (DGB, 1989). The proposals were similarly rejected by the churches, by Liselotte Funcke and by the Berlin Commissioner for Foreigners' Affairs, Barbara John, herself a CDU member, who all criticised the linking of both entry for dependants and unlimited residence permits to adequate living space (Beauftragte der Bundesregierung, 1989b; Franz, 1990). Strong reservations were expressed over the proposed time-scale for the reform. The DGB recommended shelving the proposal until after the 1990 election so that it could be scrutinised thoroughly (DGB, 1989), while Liselotte Funcke expressed the hope that the Interior Ministry would take account of the various suggestions before sending the bill to cabinet and hence to parliament (Beauftragte der Bundesregierung, 1989b).

This general feeling of scepticism was echoed on 20 October 1989, when the draft was presented to a number of interest groups in a consultation exercise at the Interior Ministry. These included the welfare organisations, churches, the UNHCR, as well as unions and employers, but notably no representatives of foreigners' groups. While all the groups present agreed that the general aims of the law were good, the specific proposals met with broad and sustained criticism from every group except the employers (Bundestagsdrucksache 11/6321). Significantly, a further high-level discussion took place between Interior Minister Schäuble and the Chairman of the Catholic Bishops' Conference (the *Deutsche Bischofskonferenz*), Karl Lehmann, on 19 November 1989. Lehmann too welcomed elements of the draft, notably the formal regulation of family reunification, but voiced concerns over several of the law's other provisions, for instance the sections pertaining to expulsion (Deutscher Bundestag Innenausschuss, 1990: 341–2).

Although the draft was amended to include some of the points raised, its key provisions remained unchanged in their essence. Yet despite the overt reservations from the interest organisations, which in some cases peaked in outright opposition, the federal cabinet agreed to move ahead on 13 December 1989, presenting it as a government bill to parliament immediately after the Christmas recess.

Formulation and legislation

The rapid pace of reform set in late 1989 was not only maintained in early 1990, but stepped up significantly. On 5 January 1990, the federal government sent the bill for the new *Ausländergesetz* (Bundestagsdrucksache 11/6321) to the *Bundesrat* as an urgent measure (*besonders eilbedürftig*), which meant it could be introduced into the *Bundestag* even before the *Bundesrat's* comments had been received.[2] Indeed, when the *Bundesrat* did deliver its opinion on 16 February 1990 (Bundestagsdrucksache 11/6541), it was one week *after* the bill's first reading in the *Bundestag* and two days *after* the Interior Affairs Select Committee had held a special public hearing on the bill.

By the time of the first plenary reading of the bill on 9 February 1990, five weeks after the formal beginning of the legislative process, all hopes of exhaustive discussion leading to a broad cross-party consensus had evaporated, just as Barwig (1989) had predicted. The ensuing debate illustrated the polarised nature of the party political positions between government and opposition, as well as the determination of the coalition partners to drive through the compromise that had been reached (Deutscher Bundestag Plenarprotokoll 11/195).

Following its first reading, the bill was forwarded to the relevant select committees for consideration, with the Interior Affairs Select Committee (*Innenausschuss*) taking overall responsibility.[3] The committee already had before it a number of other bills from the government and the opposition parties in this area, some dating back to 1988. In line with normal practice, these were bundled together into a batch of eight bills and three motions for the committee to deal with together. Given the bill's complexity and importance, a public hearing was scheduled for 14 February 1990, at which various interest groups and individual experts (*Sachverständige*) were invited to present their assessment of the proposals.

The fact that this hearing was scheduled for only five days after the bill's first reading gives some idea of the sense of urgency involved, certainly on the side of the government coalition. This haste becomes particularly clear when one considers the fact that the date of the hearing had been agreed between the parties on 14 December 1989, just one day after being signed off by the federal cabinet (Deutscher Bundestag Plenarprotokoll 11/207: 16273). Moreover, the very tight schedule meant that the written submissions were sent to the *Bundestag* only between seven and ten days before the actual hearing. Given that these alone consisted of 490 pages in the minutes, and were of a highly complex and legalistic nature, it is unlikely that the committee members were able to examine the submissions with the due care and attention the significance of the bill arguably merited.

The hearing itself was instructive for understanding the bill's legislation, in so far as it highlighted both the concerns over the law and the degree to which these concerns were subsequently ignored. A broad range of individuals and organisations was called upon to give evidence:

- Representatives of local government organisations (*Deutscher Städtetag, Deutscher Städte- und Gemeindebund, Deutscher Landkreistag*)

- Representatives of the local and regional administrative levels, who would implement the new law

- Lawyers and judges at the administrative courts, who would supervise the law's implementation

- Societal interest groups, including the unions, the two Christian churches, the welfare organisation and Barbara John, the Berlin Commissioner for Foreigners' Affairs

- As a number of the bills dealt with asylum seekers and refugees, Amnesty International, Terre des Hommes, the UNHCR and Lufthansa were invited to give evidence

- Finally, of the over twenty submissions, only one was from a representative of the Turkish community.

The hearing itself appears to have been extremely complex, at times emotionally charged, yet at other times very dull: many of the interventions were turned into mini-speeches and make for ungainly reading. The quality of contributions also varied greatly and in one case bordered on the frivolous. For instance, Professor Harald Fliegauf, the 'representative of Baden-Württemberg's public interest' (his official title) and a CDU/CSU nominee, declined to give a written submission, preferring instead to ground his oral 'expert opinion' to a considerable extent on information contained in newspaper reports. He singled out the proposed regulation of family reunification for particular criticism, noting that this represented a major gap in Germany's defences against immigration. Indeed, he suggested that foreigners who married partners from their country of origin should be expected to return there, as this clearly demonstrated the immigrant's lack of commitment to Germany. He attempted to underline his argument by pointing out that Germany's infrastructure, including explicitly its road network, was in no situation to cope with a further influx of immigrants (Deutscher Bundestag Innenausschuss, 1990: 8, 256–7).

Most of the other contributions undertook a somewhat better informed and detailed critique of the bill's contents. But there was little agreement. Submissions by the executive tended to welcome the bill, while most of the lawyers present harboured a greater or lesser degree of reservation. By contrast, the submissions by the welfare organisations, the unions, the churches, by Barbara John and Hakki Keskin who, as representative of the Turkish community in Hamburg was the only foreigner invited, were overwhelmingly critical of the bill. Most of its regulations, including the sections on entry, residence, refugee and naturalisation, were rejected as being too harsh, or as sending the wrong signals to the foreign population. It was scant compensation, then, that some contributions from societal groups also noted how much the bill had improved since the 1988 proposals.

Although the bill was before the committee for over ten weeks, its deliberations were sporadic. Having been on the agenda on 17 January 1990, even before its first reading, the bill was deliberated in committee only on 7, 14, 28 and 29 March, as well as on 23 April 1990 (Bundestagsdrucksache 11/6960: 3). However, the suggestions of the expert witnesses received little consideration. In particular, the views of the societal groups, who constituted the most critical section of the experts, were, in effect, ignored. The *Bundesrat*, which finally issued its opinion on 16 February 1990, having used the full six weeks available to it for discussion, fared little better. It proposed a total of forty-six amendments, most of which were editorial, as well as one more significant suggestion: the *Bundesrat* proposed raising the age limit for the 'simplified naturalisation' procedure from twenty-one to twenty-three and establishing this as a legal right (*Rechtsanspruch*). While the federal government agreed with many of these either in whole or in part, seventeen of the *Bundesrat's* suggestions were rejected outright (Bundestagsdrucksache 11/6541).

In total, the Interior Affairs Select Committee considered some 200 amendments to the bill. Nonetheless, its final recommendations, published on 24 April 1990 (Bundestagsdrucksachen 11/6955 and 11/6960), bore a very close resemblance to the original draft. Those amendments which were adopted, mainly those proposed by the CDU/CSU and FDP, were mostly cosmetic or constituted a clarification of the original text. In only a few cases were meaningful changes made. For instance, the prerequisite of adequate living space for family reunification was relaxed slightly and the age limit for simplified naturalisation was raised to twenty-three, although this was not formulated, as the *Bundesrat* had suggested, as a general legal entitlement. By far the most significant amendment came with the extension of the new simplified naturalisation procedure to first-generation immigrants who had lived in Germany for over fifteen years. This idea had first been mooted by SPD-led *Länder* during the course of the 1983 commission, and while it had been rejected by the CDU/CSU at the time, its inclusion in the *Ausländergesetz* bill represents the only case where a significant opposition proposal found its way into the bill. The calculation was that by the time the offer expired (31 December 1995), between 75 per cent and 90 per cent of all foreigners over the age of thirty-five would qualify (Bundestagsdrucksache 11/6960: 28). The SPD's and Greens' other amendments, inevitably, found little support outside their own ranks.

By the time the bill returned to the floor of the *Bundestag*, the style of legislative procedure had been set. The process had taken place at breakneck speed, with scant regard for the conventions of consensus between government and opposition normally associated with German politics. Instead, an unashamedly majoritarian approach had been taken by the coalition partners and this was continued during what turned out to be the final day of debate in the *Bundestag*. The Interior Affairs Select Committee had concluded its deliberations at midday on 23 April 1990. Without waiting for the Judicial Affairs Committee (*Rechtsausschuss*), the main secondary committee examining the bill, to deliver its recommendations, the CDU/CSU applied to include the combined second and third readings of the bill on the parliamentary agenda of the first available plenary session just three days later, on Thursday 26 April 1990.

When the *Bundestag* assembled that morning to consider this motion, the degree of frustration caused by the effective exclusion of the opposition SPD and Greens from the committee stage quickly became apparent (Deutscher Bundestag Plenarprotokoll 11/207: 16203–6). As one SPD member, Jahn, put it to the ruling coalition during the debate of the CDU/CSU's procedural motions at the beginning of that day: 'nobody is denying you [the CDU/CSU–FDP] the right to use your majority as you see fit. But no majority has the right to dogmatically exploit its formal powers' (Deutscher Bundestag Plenarprotokoll 11/207: 16204).

For the CDU/CSU, its interior affairs spokesman, Johannes Gerster, justified the combination of the second and third readings of the bill by arguing that the debates over a new law had gone on for years and that the bill was ready to be passed. In a rather glib defence of the bill's swift progress, he pointed out that the opposition had, during the committee's final session that Monday, given up at midday, rather than continuing through until midnight, and that it had refused to debate the bill on Good Friday. In retaliation, the SPD accused the ruling coalition of systematically refusing to discuss and debate the various proposals, in particular the objections and reservations raised by the societal interest groups at the hearing in February. The opposition lost the vote and the bill's combined second and third readings were scheduled for later on that afternoon.[4]

In the light of the heated emotions the bill and its handling had provoked previously, it is perhaps not surprising that the final debate turned out to be an ill-tempered affair (Deutscher Bundestag Plenarprotokoll 11/207: 16269–301). It was marred by personal insults and even resulted in two Green members being expelled from the chamber. The SPD again fiercely criticised the government, not only for the content of the bill, but also for following up years of debate and discussion, both formal and informal, with just a three-month-long period for parliamentary consideration. In particular, its speakers accused the government of pushing the bill through before the *Land* election in Lower Saxony on 13 May 1990. The debate was followed by no fewer than twenty-one votes by three-line whip (*namentliche Abstimmungen*), twenty of which had been called for by the Greens. As was to be expected, the government won all of them.

With the *Bundestag*'s consent secured, the bill passed back to the *Bundesrat*. Here the opposition staged a last-ditch attempt to prevent the bill from being passed. In its meeting on 2 May 1990, the *Bundesrat*'s own Interior Affairs Committee recommended that a decision be postponed: it simply had not had enough time to examine the bill in detail (Deutscher Bundesrat Plenarprotokoll 290/1/90). But it was to no avail: the CDU/CSU *Länder* were determined to push the bill through while their majority was still guaranteed. On 11 May 1990, the *Bundesrat* voted in favour. Two days later, on 13 May 1990, the CDU/CSU lost its majority in that chamber through its defeat in the Lower Saxony *Land* election.

Semisovereignty and the *Ausländergesetz*

The new *Ausländergesetz*, which came into force on 1 January 1991, is an immensely complex piece of legislation. Because of the political aim of replacing the brushstroke terms of the 1965 *Ausländergesetz* with definite and clear criteria, the original bill contained no fewer than 102 sections, as well as changes to a further fourteen existing laws to ensure coherence. Even Interior Minister Schäuble had to admit in the debate on 26 April 1990 that: 'The text of the bill – and this is not one of its strengths – is not easy to understand, neither for Germans, nor evidently for members of this House [the *Bundestag*], and certainly not for our foreign fellow citizens' (Deutscher Bundestag Plenarprotokoll 11/207: 16283). Its legislation marks the end of a long and acrimonious process of reform, which had first been started back in 1982, under the Schmidt government. In the seven years that followed, Interior Minister Zimmermann concentrated on all issues of *Ausländerpolitik* except the crucial area of improving the legal circumstances for foreigners' residence. As late as 1988, the Interior Ministry was proposing further, much tougher restrictions in this area. The hostile reaction these proposals received showed just how much out of synch the Interior Ministry and the CSU was with both the FDP and the moderate wings of the CDU in its conceptions of *Ausländerpolitik*.

This meant that, for most of the 1980s, the new *Ausländergesetz* was simply too hot a political potato to handle. Instead, Interior Minister Zimmermann's refusal to build a sustainable compromise on anything other than his terms (as laid out in the 1988 draft) constitutes a first clear example of non-decision-making in this policy area. That this was a conscious decision on Zimmermann's part is confirmed by Wolfgang Schäuble in his memoirs:

> Fritz Zimmermann, my predecessor as Interior Minister, had felt that a proper reform of the legal framework for non-nationals was impossible, given what he saw as a lack of consensus within the coalition over the basic elements of such a reform. As a result, he declined to propose a formal bill. (Schäuble, 2001: 77)

It took a number of exogenous factors to create a climate in which a reform could be tackled. First, Zimmermann was replaced in 1989 by the more emollient Schäuble as Interior Minister. Second, the success of right-wing parties that same year made it necessary to draw a line under the question of reform before the series of important elections

due in 1990. Third, the likelihood that the government might lose its
Bundesrat majority at the Lower Saxony election in May 1990 undoubtedly helped concentrate minds, within both the conservative and
liberal sections of Chancellor Kohl's coalition. It is worth noting that
had elite conceptions of *Ausländerpolitik* been homogeneous, as Brubaker (1992) implies they are, then a reform would surely have taken
place much earlier.

How, though, does this case study reflect semisovereign patterns of
policy-making in West Germany? In fact, the genesis and development
of the 1990 *Ausländergesetz* can clearly be explained in the context of
the semisovereign model of governance. Indeed, many of the features
of Katzenstein's model can be identified from the events described
above, even if the precise constellation of political forces, as noted in
Chapter 1, does differ somewhat from other policy areas.

First of all, the decentralisation of state power is particularly visible:
throughout the period in question, no single governmental actor was
able to impose either a liberal or a conservative agenda onto policy.
The SPD-led *Länder* of Hamburg and Schleswig-Holstein, thanks to the
1990 ruling of the Constitutional Court on this matter, were unable to
grant local voting rights to foreigners. At the same time, the highly
conservative Interior Minister Zimmermann singularly failed to make
any headway with two key political projects, the reduction in the
maximum age for *Kindernachzug* from sixteen to six and the tightening
of residence law exemplified by the 1988 proposals. Despite his formal
responsibility for this policy area (the *Ressortprinzip*), he was unable to
hold out against widespread criticism of both sets of proposals. Neither
was he helped by the Constitutional Court's relatively liberal rulings on
family reunification policy in the late 1980s.

Moreover, even though interest groups such as the unions and churches resolutely opposed Zimmermann's propositions, they had lost most
of their leverage by the early 1980s with the transformation of *Ausländerpolitik* from a labour market into a public order issue. In consequence,
they can take little credit for torpedoing his agenda. Instead, it was
coalition politics and the diverse range of opinions within the CDU
which proved to be Zimmermann's most effective opponents. Thus
the CDU's social-catholic wing was instrumental in making the 1988
Interior Ministry proposals politically untenable. An equally important
role was played by the junior coalition partner, the FDP: its senior
minister, Foreign Minister Hans-Dietrich Genscher, made a number of
personal interventions during the 1980s to prevent Zimmermann's

plans for a more restrictive *Ausländerpolitik* (O'Brien, 1996: 85; also Joppke, 1999: 82). Coalition politics thus helped to exercise a definite centripetal influence on an otherwise hardline CDU and CSU during the 1980s.

The federal coalition would also prove to be the forum where the eventual policy compromise was struck and pushed through. Yet it was possible to carry this compromise through parliament only because the SPD held no veto position in the *Bundesrat* and because of the comparatively weak role interest groups have in this policy sector. Had the churches and unions been indispensable for the successful implementation of the law, their influence would have been correspondingly greater.

Second, despite there being no significant parapublic institutions in this policy field at the time, the other two nodes of the network are still clearly visible. For instance, the exigencies of cooperative federalism prevented the 1983 federation–*Länder* commission from coming up with anything more dramatic in *Ausländerpolitik* than the formalisation of existing administrative practices. But in particular, it is political parties which stand out, not only as one of the nodes of the network, but also as policy-making institutions in their own right. In the absence of parapublic institutions and of powerful insider societal interests in this field, the coalition parties quickly filled the void to become the principal counterpart to the Interior Ministry's technical expertise in this area. This became particularly clear following the 1988 controversy over the Interior Ministry's drafts, after which the coalition's parliamentary parties (*Fraktionen*) took on a much more central role. For instance, even before Zimmermann left the Interior Ministry in 1989, the coalition parties' interior spokesmen had been charged by the Federal Chancellery with the formulation of the *Eckwerte* paper, thereby explicitly, and unusually, undermining the *Ressortprinzip*.

Later on in the process, the *Bundestag*'s Interior Affairs Select Committee made some small, but hugely significant alterations to the bill. As noted above, the committee not only raised the age limit for simplified naturalisation for second-generation foreigners from twenty-one to twenty-three, but also extended the whole concept to (usually first-generation) foreigners with over fifteen years' residence in Germany (Bundestagsdrucksache 11/6955). In light of the fact that the latter accounted for the majority of simplified naturalisations since they began to be recorded separately in 1993 (Beauftragte der Bundesregierung, 2002), this amendment has had an appreciable impact on the foreign population. The *Fraktionen* therefore played a defining role in the formulation of the law: as a (limited) counterweight to the technical expertise of the Interior Ministry, as the forum where the main compromise (the *Eckwerte* paper) was reached and as actors in their own right during the legislative process. Perhaps understandably, this appears not to have been popular within the Interior Ministry: Johannes Gerster, the CDU/CSU's interior spokesman and one of the authors of the *Eckwerte* paper, implied that the degree of control exercised by the coalition parties had caused friction with the Interior Ministry by conceding in parliament that its officials had not always been easy to work with (Deutscher Bundestag Plenarprotokoll 11/207: 16292–3).

Ultimately, and most importantly in terms of the validity of the model of semisovereign governance, the outcome of this long and complicated reform process was one of incremental policy change. In purely formal terms, the new *Ausländergesetz* certainly represented a significant change compared to the 1965 version, but this ignores the fact that most of its provisions constituted the codification of established administrative practice. Indeed, most of these changes had already been foreshadowed in the discussions of the 1983 commission on *Ausländer-politik*. Even the introduction of the simplified naturalisation procedure, at least for second-generation foreigners, had been discussed by the commission (Haberland, 1983: 60–1). Moreover, as Chapter 4 will show, its effect was not as far-reaching as might at first have been assumed. When all was said and done, the constellation of interests and power within the coalition meant that no substantial departure from estab-lished practice in either a more liberal or restrictive direction was possible. The new *Ausländergesetz* thus effectively embodied the path dependency that the 1977 and 1983 commissions on *Ausländerpolitik* had set in motion.

It is also worth dwelling briefly on the highly confrontational style in which the law was passed, which bears greater resemblance to the adversarial 'Westminster' style of politics than the traditionally more measured path towards consensus in German politics. Once the window of opportunity for reforming the law had been identified, the analysis of the legislative process shows that all available procedural tools were used to see the bill through as quickly and with as few concessions to the opposition as possible. In consequence, there is little evidence of the negotiation relationship, especially with regard to societal actors, which Dyson (1982) identifies as the preferred form in the search for policy solutions in Germany. The numerous consultations with societal interests that did take place were, with hindsight, superficial: the concerns of unions, churches and welfare organisations, as well as practically all the SPD's suggestions for improvement, were summarily dismissed, not least because any concessions would potentially have unravelled the lowest-common-denominator agreement between the coalition parties. This explicitly majoritarian approach set a pattern of parliamentary procedure in *Ausländerpolitik* which was to be repeated in both the other case studies to be examined in this book.

In conclusion, the formulation of the *Ausländergesetz* can be seen to both confirm and modify the semisovereign model of governance. While incremental outcomes remain the default result of policy, the lack of a negotiated settlement and the deep party political conflict over *Ausländerpolitik* from 1982 highlights the limits of consensus politics. The case study also modifies the notion of the semisovereignty of the state: with a sympathetic *Bundesrat* majority and ineffectual interest groups, the pace and content of reform was determined solely by the point at which deep-seated disagreements both between and within the CDU/CSU–FDP coalition could be resolved, a process in which exogenous electoral factors also played a key role. The instance of semisovereignty, therefore, was the federal coalition, rather than the pantheon of policy-making actors more generally. Moreover, once an agreement had been reached over the basic content of the law, the government and its parliamentary parties sidelined all objections from the opposition parties, whose approval was not formally needed to pass the bill, or from any of the concerned interest groups, who were only tangential to the implementation of the law. As Chapters 4 and 5 will show, such a constellation of power was not to be repeated during the 1990s.

Two postscripts must be added to this case study. First, the government's highly respected Commissioner for Foreigners' Affairs, Liselotte Funcke, resigned in January 1991 over the content of the new law. Second, the controversy over the law was to drag on well into the 1990s, as it took an astonishing eight years for the federal government and the *Bundesrat*, which was by now controlled by the SPD, to reach agreement on the law's secondary legislation (*allgemeine Verwaltungsvorschriften*). This was a rare example of disagreements over more technical matters of policy, but at the same time illustrated the total lack of consensus over citizenship that was to dominate *Ausländerpolitik* during Chancellor Kohl's last four years in office. This will be the main focus of Chapter 4.

Notes

1 The Justice Ministry is required to examine all bills for their compatibility with existing legislation (*Rechtsförmlichkeitsprüfung*). However, because the ministry was in FDP hands during the Kohl era, such ostensibly administrative discussions often also had a political sub-agenda, sounding out areas of consensus and conflict between the FDP and the CDU/CSU-led ministries.

2 Article 76 of the Basic Law lays down the standard legislative procedure in Germany, under which the *Bundesrat* is required to be consulted on all bills before they are considered by the *Bundestag*: the *Bundesrat* may take up to nine weeks for this. However, if a bill is classified as urgent (*besonders eilbedürftig*), the federal government may introduce the bill into the *Bundestag* after only three weeks, even if the *Bundesrat* has not yet delivered its initial opinion, which is required within six weeks. This procedure, therefore, considerably shortens the time necessary for parliamentary scrutiny.

3 This is normal procedure in Germany's legislative process: contested votes are not normally held until the second or third reading of a bill.

4 Normally, the *Bundestag* can vote to combine the second and third readings of a bill only with a two-thirds majority. However, if a bill is classified as urgent by the government, as was the case here, a simple majority suffices.

4

The reform of citizenship policy, 1990–99

The new *Ausländergesetz*, which came into force on 1 January 1991, completed the legal institutionalisation of the *de facto* residence framework for non-nationals that had been in place since 1978. As well as providing clear entitlements to secure residence permits and the main elements of family reunification, the law took a tentative but significant step towards recognising that West Germany's previous naturalisation policy, as elaborated in the 1977 Guidelines on Naturalisation, was failing to promote the legal inclusion via citizenship of the country's foreign population. The new, 'simplified naturalisation' procedure in the *Ausländergesetz* was intended to address this problem by promising naturalisation 'as a rule' for two groups: foreigners with over fifteen years' residence, and foreigners aged between sixteen and twenty-three with over eight years' residence and six years' attendance of a German school. In both cases, naturalisation was subject to the applicant being released from his/her former citizenship. While the cost for 'normal' naturalisations under the 1913 *Reichs- und Staatsangehörigkeitsgesetz* (RuStAG) remained high (up to DM 5,000), the fees for simplified naturalisations were set at just DM 100 (details in Green, 2001b).

This new, twin-tracked system of naturalisation under the either the RuStAG or the *Ausländergesetz* certainly helped to increase access to citizenship: the annual naturalisation rate of the non-national population (excluding ethnic Germans, who continued to account for the majority of total naturalisations) trebled from 0.4 per cent in 1990 to 1.2 per cent in 1996, rising further to 2.0 per cent in 1999. Much of this increase can be attributed to a considerably higher level of naturalisations among the Turkish population, which in 1999 accounted for over 70 per cent of all non-ethnic German naturalisations. From 1993 onwards, its naturalisation rate has exceeded that of the foreign population as a whole, peaking in 1999, when an impressive 5 per cent of Turkish nationals in Germany received German citizenship (see Appendix). This increase is all the more important because EU nationals, who account for around one-quarter of all foreign residents in Germany, have very little incentive to naturalise, given that they enjoy security of residence and access to the labour market equal to that of Germans. As in other EU countries, their naturalisation rates are very low.

However, the undoubted positive impact of the 1990 *Ausländergesetz* on access to citizenship must be qualified in two principal areas. First, the starting point in absolute terms is so low (a mere 20,000 naturalisations in 1990) that even these increased numbers have made little impression on the goal of reducing the overall total of foreigners in Germany identified by the Kohl government in 1984. Put bluntly, the increased number of naturalisations was not high enough to compensate for the combined impact of continued high net immigration levels throughout the 1990s (with the exception of 1997 and 1998), and of demographics. Not only was the birth rate among non-nationals higher than among Germans, but lower average age of non-nationals meant that there was little natural population decrease through mortality: in 1999, there were almost seven times more live births than deaths of non-nationals (Beauftragte der Bundesregierung, 2002: 266, 295). The cumulated impact of net immigration, citizenship policy and demographics has meant that the total number of foreigners in Germany has remained more or less static at around 7.3 million, or about 8.9 per cent of the population, ever since 1998. It is sobering to note that the naturalisation rate in comparable European countries, such as France, the UK and especially the Netherlands, has consistently been higher than in Germany, in addition to which all three countries traditionally operate *ius soli*.[1]

Second, it is misleading to conclude that the high number of Turkish citizens naturalised in the late 1990s is solely due to an increased level of interest in German citizenship among this group. Rather, the Turkish government in 1999 managed to clear a large backlog of applications for release from its citizenship, each of which had to be approved individually by the prime minister until a change in regulations in the late 1990s (Interview C). This also helps explain why the naturalisation rate for Turks actually decreased to what is by implication a more normal level between 1999 and 2002.

In its effect, therefore, the simplified naturalisation procedure was little more than incremental, and puts the quadrupling in the absolute number of naturalisations of non-nationals between 1990 and 1996 in a somewhat different light. It also means that this policy innovation failed to resolve the paradox of ever-increasing average residence times, especially among the former guestworkers, and parallel legal marginalisation and exclusion from the political process (cf. Rubio-Marin, 2000). At the same time, and despite the fact that most social and civil citizenship rights were already available to non-nationals (Soysal, 1994), citizenship remained a decisive instance of exclusion, especially for non-EU nationals. For as well as providing security of residence and full political rights, German nationality is a prerequisite for many senior-, middle- and even some junior-ranking positions in public service (*Beamte*), including judges, civil servants, public prosecutors, university professors and teachers. Consequently, there are very few people of non-German origin to be found in such positions.

With the Constitutional Court in 1990 closing off the route of granting any political rights to non-EU nationals, naturalisation remained the only route available for bringing Germany's ever-more settled non-national population into the fold of the political community. The parties were certainly already aware of this in the 1980s, but at the time there was little agreement over the policy options, not least because a full-scale reform of citizenship was precluded by the continued existence of the GDR (Green, 2000, 2001a).

It was not until the early 1990s and after unification that the policy fault lines crystallised out, which revolved around three main policy issues:

- Whether the territorial principle of ascription (*ius soli*) should be introduced in order to provide citizenship automatically to the second and subsequent generations of non-nationals

- Whether the residence requirement for simplified naturalisation of first-generation non-nationals should be reduced from its level of fifteen years in the 1990 *Ausländergesetz*

- Whether dual and multiple citizenships should continue to be rejected in naturalisations, which would necessarily also mean the rejection of *ius soli*.[2]

Within each of these three issues, the CDU/CSU adopted broadly conservative positions (against dual citizenship and *ius soli*, and preferring more modest reductions in the residence requirement for naturalisation), consistent with the notion that Germany was not a country of immigration. By contrast, the SPD and Greens, and to a lesser extent the FDP, proposed more fundamental changes (Murray, 1994).

Of these, dual citizenship was clearly the most controversial issue. As well as its relatively recent formalisation in citizenship law, Germany's rejection of dual citizenship has also been one of the key factors behind its very low naturalisation rate. In addition to the emotional dimension of being forced to give up one's citizenship of birth, there have been real material disincentives to take into consideration: for instance, Turkish citizens until 1995 lost their inheritance rights if they gave up their citizenship and Turkish youths have been required to pay high fees to release them from their obligations of military service (Thrän-hardt, 2000: 143). In particular, the requirement to be released from one's citizenship has the effect of considerably lengthening the admin-istrative process of naturalisation, not least because a range of countries, including Turkey and Iran, have been either technically unable or simply unwilling to release their nationals (*Der Spiegel*, 7 July 1997). Yet from the German perspective, the onus usually remained on the applicant to persevere in his or her attempts to obtain release. Only when the *Land* to which the application had been made decided that the country of origin was deliberately slowing up the release could dual citizenship be tolerated.[3] With no secondary legislation for the *Ausländergesetz* for most of the 1990s, the *Länder* have been free to interpret this and other provisions as they see fit, leading to a considerable divergence between states in both naturalisation rates and in the proportion of naturalisations tolerating dual citizenship (Hagedorn, 2001: 157–8). When combined with varying administrative resources available locally, processing times of two to three years and longer have not been uncommon (cf. Hagedorn, 2001: 58–61). As if this was not enough, it was standard practice for countries such as Yugoslavia to charge its citizens eye-watering release fees of up to several thousand Deutschmarks.

The impact of Germany's principled rejection of dual citizenship on processing times for naturalisation is particularly important because opinion research from 1993 clearly showed that the bureaucratic com-plexity of naturalisation was the single biggest reason for non-application among foreigners interested in German citizenship (quoted in Hagedorn, 2001: 159). In terms of actually making headway with the naturalisation of Germany's most settled non-nationals, there can be little doubt that the general acceptance of dual citizenship, together with the introduction of *ius soli*, would have been the most effective policy instruments, especially if backed up by a much higher level of information to non-nationals. But the political debate over citizenship reform throughout the 1990s was rarely concerned with finding the most rational policy solution in order to achieve an aim on which all parties in fact agreed. Instead, disputes were again dominated by largely symbolic issues such as national identity and integration, as well as by the perennial question of whether Germany was a country of immigration.

While the parties' different conceptions of integration will be returned to in Chapter 5, the purpose of this chapter is to analyse and discuss how this issue of citizenship reform was ultimately resolved by 1 January 2000, when Germany's first new citizenship law in eighty-six years came into force. Just as had been the case with the reform of the *Ausländergesetz* in the 1980s, the process of passing a new citizenship law took several years, and moreover depended on the first ever full-scale change of government following a parliamentary election (Green, 1999). More significantly in the context of this analysis, the semisovereign structure of the German state is absolutely crucial in explaining both when the reform ultimately came about and what its content was. As this chapter will show, the German political system's tendency to reach 'non-decisions' in the case of severe political conflict neatly explains why, contrary to all promises by the government, no reform was enacted between the 1994 and 1998 *Bundestag* elections. In addition, political parties, acting as nodes of the policy-making network, explicitly employed the structures of federalism to limit the reach of the SPD–Green government's reform proposals in early 1999.

However, as before, the chapter will begin by placing this debate in the context of other developments in the 1990s, especially unification and the asylum crisis of 1992 and 1993.

Ausländerpolitik and unification

Initially, unification between East and West Germany on 3 October 1990 appeared to have no significant effect on *Ausländerpolitik*. West Germany's former guestworker generation was now reasonably well settled and the new *Ausländergesetz*, which came into force on 1 January 1991, undoubtedly improved the framework for its residence. At the same time, unification itself added few new non-national residents to the population: although the GDR too had recruited guestworkers mainly from socialist countries such as Vietnam and Mozambique, it had never done so on the scale of the West. In 1989, there were only 94,000 guestworkers in the country, around half of the total non-national population of 190,000 in that year (Gruner-Domiç, 1999). In 2001, over 95 per cent of non-nationals in Germany still lived in the 'old' *Länder* of western Germany plus Berlin. As an issue, *Ausländerpolitik* was therefore drowned out in the general euphoria over unification and played no meaningful role in the first all-German *Bundestag* election of 2 December 1990, at which the *Republikaner* party, despite its successes of the previous year, failed to make a significant impact.

Asylum and ethnic German immigration, 1991–93

However, the calm quickly proved deceptive. The simultaneous end of the Cold War and the collapse of Yugoslavia at the beginning of the 1990s was to transform Germany's immigration and citizenship policy. With east–west travel suddenly possible, literally hundreds of thousands of ethnic Germans and asylum seekers arrived in Germany from the late 1980s onwards to start new lives (see Table 3.1 on p. 55 and Appendix). These migrations peaked in 1990 and 1992, when almost 400,000 ethnic Germans and over 438,000 asylum seekers, respectively, arrived in Germany. In response, a law in 1990 (the *Aussiedleraufnahmegesetz*) imposed procedural restrictions on the ethnic Germans' hitherto un-limited right to immigration. From 1997 onwards, entry to Germany was also made conditional on the successful completion of language tests.

With such huge numbers of arrivals, it was unsurprising that immi-gration, and most of all asylum, returned to preoccupy the public's mind. By late 1992, fears that 'the boat is full' (*Das Boot ist voll*) were reflected in opinion polls, with record levels of respondents in the *Politbarometer* polls considering the issue of 'asylum and foreigners' to be important (Forschungsgruppe Wahlen, 2000). Now extreme right-wing parties were once again able to capitalise on public concern: in each of the *Land* elections in Bremen in September 1991 and in Baden-Württemberg and Schleswig-Holstein in April 1992, either the German Peoples' Union (*Deutsche Volksunion*, DVU) or the *Republi-kaner* scored over 5 per cent. More worryingly, recorded racially motivated attacks on foreigners more than doubled from 2,426 in 1991 to 6,336 in 1992. In September 1991 and August 1992, major anti-foreigner riots in the eastern German towns of Hoyerswerda and

Rostock, respectively, dominated headlines, particularly in the international media. A tragic zenith was reached in the firebombing of Turkish families in Mölln on 23 November 1992 and in Solingen on 29 May 1993, which together cost the lives of eight people. In the shock that followed the murders in Mölln, hundreds of thousands of ordinary citizens lined the streets of German cities in candle-lit vigils (*Lichterketten*) against xenophobia during December 1992.

By this time, the search for a political solution in the form of an amendment of the constitutionally enshrined entitlement to asylum was in full flow. Already in 1991, Chancellor Kohl had attempted to pre-empt the domestic debate by pushing for a solution at European level (Henson and Malhan, 1995). However, with little chance of success in the face of British intransigence over the supranational integration of such a sensitive policy area, the question returned to the domestic arena in 1992. The CDU/CSU argued that the flow of asylum seekers could be cut off only by a change to the Basic Law. In doing so, the party knew it spoke for the public mood: in February 1992's *Politbarometer*, 67 per cent in the west and 74 per cent in the east favoured such a constitutional amendment (Forschungsgruppe Wahlen, 2000).

However, this required a two-thirds majority in both houses of parliament, which could only be forged together with the SPD. But the SPD's misgivings over such a project were substantial: for the party's left-wingers in particular, the Basic Law's asylum provision was non-negotiable, because it explicitly represented Germany's obligations arising from its Nazi past. The Greens, too, refused to contemplate this proposal and as a result, a political stalemate quickly ensued.

Meanwhile, public and political pressure on the SPD was mounting. Already, all the main parties had come under sustained attack by the media for their apparent failure to cooperate in addressing the concerns of voters over immigration. Allensbach (IfD) polls in October 1991 and December 1992 showed that over 60 per cent of the electorate felt that politicians were not seriously trying to find a solution to the problem (IfD polls 5056, 5074). The mounting violence during 1992 and successes of extremist parties in previous elections further fuelled the feeling that 'something needs to be done'. The 'non-decision' option was therefore no longer politically sustainable for the SPD.

The CDU/CSU exploited this public concern effectively. Following its highly unpopular U-turn in early 1991 on its 1990 election promise to finance unification without raising taxes, it sensed an opportunity to regain the political initiative from the SPD. Its general secretary, Volker

Rühe, instructed all party branches in 1991 to push the asylum issue at every opportunity: the SPD was to be portrayed as the single obstacle in the path of reforming asylum law, and thereby reducing unwanted immigration.

Pressure for reform was mounting from within the SPD, too. Although the party's left-wing and intellectuals such as Günter Grass passionately opposed the proposed amendment (Grass later symbolically left the party as a result), its right-wing, organised in the Seeheimer Circle, pushed for a change of policy on electoral grounds: the CDU/CSU had clearly caught the SPD on the hop, and with nineteen regional and federal elections due in 1994 alone, the party could ill afford to be seen as out of touch with public opinion on a matter as crucial as this. Polls continued to show a large majority in favour of a constitutional amendment: in October 1992, a FORSA survey (948/2356) showed not only that 62 per cent of the population favoured asylum reform, but that 57 per cent of the SPD's own voters also supported this proposal. After much soul-searching, the SPD leader, Björn Engholm, finally managed to secure the agreement of his party to a reform in November 1992.

The formal agreement between the CDU/CSU, FDP and SPD followed on 6 December 1992, in the immediate aftermath of the Mölln murders and went beyond a mere reform of asylum provisions. In return for its support for an amendment of the Basic Law, the SPD negotiated a comprehensive package of immigration policies with the CDU/CSU and the FDP, which specifically included ethnic German immigration and citizenship policy. The compromise thus contained three main points:

- Asylum seekers from 'safe countries' or from 'safe third countries' (in particular EU member-states and countries on Germany's eastern border) would be automatically rejected. Moreover, a 'fast-track' applications procedure was to be instituted at airports.

- Ethnic German immigration would be subjected to an informal annual quota of 225,000 persons. The 1992 *Kriegsfolgenbereinigungsgesetz* also limited ethnic German status to persons born before 1 January 1993 and required any new applicants from central and eastern Europe (but not from the former Soviet Union) to provide evidence of persecution on grounds of their ethnicity.

- The simplified naturalisation procedure contained in the *Ausländergesetz* was extended from a temporally limited process of 'naturalisation as a rule' (*Regelanspruch*) to a permanent entitlement to German citizenship (*Rechtsanspruch*). The fees for naturalisations under the RuStAG were also slashed to DM 500, while the government pledged to make its comprehensive reform a priority.

With the Greens, who opposed the asylum amendment, not involved in the compromise, the Basic Law was duly altered on 28 June 1993 and the new version come into effect on 1 July 1993. Perhaps predictably, the new asylum regime was later challenged in the Constitutional Court, but this ruled in May 1996 that the safe third country and safe country of origin rules did not compromise the availability of the constitutional right to asylum, thereby adding the ultimate legal seal of approval to the amendments.

In practical terms, the new provisions were reasonably effective. There were still more than 200,000 ethnic German immigrants per annum between 1992 and 1995, after which numbers did drop rapidly to stand at 91,000 in 2002, and in 1999 their immigration quota was reduced further to just over 100,000 persons annually. Simultaneously, the changes in definitions meant that the origins of ethnic German immigration shifted almost entirely towards the former Soviet Union. The impact on asylum was more dramatic, and the number of new asylum seekers fell by over 100,000 in 1993 and by a further 150,000 in 1994 (see the Appendix). But from then on, the reduction was more gradual and it was not until 1998 that new applications dipped below the 100,000 mark for the first time since 1987. Nonetheless, in both 2000 and 2002, Germany was displaced by the UK as the EU member-state with the most asylum seekers. Perhaps more importantly, levels of support for extreme right-wing parties fell rapidly, and no such party was to again achieve representation in a *Land* parliament until the Baden-Württemberg election of March 1996.

The asylum issue dominated not just *Ausländerpolitik* for almost two years, but almost the entire domestic political agenda. Spillover into other areas of *Ausländerpolitik* was therefore inevitable, and pressing issues such as citizenship reform and ethnic German immigration were subsumed in the general upheaval over asylum. Even the other elements of the comprehensive deal of 6 December 1992 received relatively little public attention. Yet while the public debate focused specifically on the issue of asylum seekers, the violence and general xenophobia that accompanied it did not. Long-term immigrants were just as likely to suffer as asylum seekers: the surviving mother of the arson attack in Mölln was tellingly captured on television, pleading that her family were neither 'asylum seekers' nor 'Kurds', but 'real Turks' (cited in Bade, 1994: 84).

Other issues during the 1990s

While asylum and (later) citizenship reform dominated the 1990s, other issues variously appeared on the policy agenda. These included attempts to prevent new immigration. In January 1997, Interior Minister Manfred Kanther announced a change in administrative regulations which required children under the age of sixteen from former guestworker recruitment countries to obtain a residence permit, a stipulation from which they had hitherto, exceptionally, been exempted. This again caused a storm of protest, although this had already been discussed in the context of the 1983 commission. As family reunification remained a major form of immigration, proposals to restrict this also reappeared periodically, especially from the CSU. In January 1998, for example, the party proposed further restrictions to allow spouses to join only immigrants holding an unlimited residence permit, thereby limiting family reunification to those granted political asylum or those who had lived in Germany for more than five years. While this proposal never had a realistic chance of being adopted, it did illustrate how controversial family reunification remained even sixteen years after being first regulated. As such, this proposal foreshadowed the return of family reunification to the political centre stage during the debate over the immigration law, which will be discussed in detail in Chapter 5.

A second issue was the arrival in Germany of temporary war refugees first from Bosnia-Herzegovina and later from Kosovo. The asylum compromise included the introduction, in Section 32a of the *Ausländergesetz*, of a special status of temporary protection for such persons. While it by definition ruled out the possibility of asylum at a later stage, the status did confer the right to work in Germany. Originally, it had been the intention to use this to permit the residence of the more than 300,000 war refugees from Bosnia-Herzegovina who arrived in Germany between 1994 and 1996. But in a rare example of the failure of cooperative federalism, differences between the federal government and the *Länder* over financial arrangements (cf. p. 21) meant that this status could not be made available to this group of immigrants. Instead, the authorities provided individual refugees only with a *Duldung*, which was not even classified as a residence permit, but as a short-term stay of deportation which could be revoked at any time.[4] Most of these temporary refugees had returned to Bosnia by the late 1990s, and in 2000, only around 37,000 remained in the country. Fortunately, by the time a further 14,000 temporary war refugees arrived from Kosovo in 1999, the dispute between the federal government and the *Länder* had been resolved, and this group was able to benefit from the temporary protection status (details in Beauftragte der Bundesregierung, 2001: 48–51).

These two issues were regularly overshadowed by the question of how to deal with perceived 'criminal' foreigners, which remained politically and socially very sensitive. Following much-publicised violent demonstrations by Kurds in 1993 and 1994, the federal government amended the *Ausländergesetz* in 1997 to make the expulsion and deportation of foreigners easier and in some cases compulsory (see Bundestagsdrucksache 13/4948). A particularly tricky case arose in the run-up to the 1998 federal election, in the form of a fourteen-year-old (and therefore criminally liable) Turkish serial young offender known as 'Mehmet'. Despite his having been born in Munich and despite his parents still living there, the Bavarian authorities were keen to underline their credentials for toughness against criminal foreigners by deporting him to Turkey. Indeed, the authorities initially attempted to deport his parents with him, not on the basis of any criminal record but for dereliction of parental duty. While the courts overturned the deportation order against his parents, 'Mehmet' was duly required to leave the country on 14 November 1998. The decision, which caused considerable controversy at the time and was vehemently criticised as blatant electioneering by the liberal press, was ultimately overturned by the Federal Administrative Court in 2002. Upon this, 'Mehmet' was permitted to return to Germany, but only after four years' enforced exile in his 'home' country (see *Migration und Bevölkerung*, November 1998 and September 2002). While the case did not in fact set a legal precedent, it did once again underline the courts' capacity to set limits on the executive's scope for action.

But by the time of the 1994 federal election, the dominant issue in *Ausländerpolitik* was undoubtedly citizenship. In this respect, the collapse of the GDR had been absolutely critical, because it removed one of the principal justifications for keeping the RuStAG on the statute books. But despite the first all-German government under Helmut Kohl after the 1990 election committing itself to further, albeit unspecified reform of naturalisation procedures, this goal was soon overtaken by events in asylum policy. Nonetheless, the SPD managed to keep citizenship on the political agenda by including it in the 1992 immigration compromise, and Chancellor Kohl confirmed the aim of overhauling the RuStAG on 16 June 1993, in a government statement following the arson attack on Turks in Solingen.

The fact that long-term resident Turks had been targeted by the murderers prompted unions, churches and foreigners themselves to suggest that dual citizenship would provide better safeguards against such attacks by encouraging more foreigners to naturalise. Indeed, the Greens organised a nation-wide petition in 1993 in favour of dual citizenship which attracted over 1 million signatures. Thus not only naturalisation, but especially dual citizenship moved into the political spotlight. But the issue separated the CDU/CSU and the opposition parties: in the aftermath of the Mölln murders, the SPD introduced bills into both the *Bundestag* and *Bundesrat* (Bundestagsdrucksache 12/4533, Bundesratsdrucksache 402/93) to permit dual citizenship, but both were rejected by the CDU/CSU–FDP coalition's majority in the *Bundestag* on 28 April 1994.

The plethora of demands for a reform of the RuStAG which accompanied the asylum debate in 1992 and 1993 failed to impress the government. One problem was that time was short: the asylum debate itself took up much of the available legislative time for interior affairs. Moreover, with passions running very high during the debate over the change of the Basic Law, few government politicians were keen to tackle another hugely controversial issue of *Ausländerpolitik* so soon before the 1994 election (cf. Schäuble, 2001: 78). A further problem was the existing legal situation itself: with citizenship policy fragmented in the *Ausländergesetz*, the RuStAG, the legislation pertaining to ethnic Germans and various pieces of secondary legislation, a comprehensive reform of the legislation would be both technically complex and time-consuming (Interview D).

The non-reform of citizenship, 1994–98

As a result, the government postponed the full reform of citizenship policy until after the 1994 election, which the incumbent CDU/CSU–FDP coalition won narrowly. In the subsequent coalition agreement, the blueprint for the new law was thrashed out. This included the replacement of naturalisations under the RuStAG and the 1977 Guidelines on Naturalisation by general legal entitlements to German citizenship, as well as a reduction in the qualifying residence periods from fifteen to ten years. The centrepiece of the reform was aimed at foreign children, by introducing a new quasi-citizenship called *Kinderstaatszugehörigkeit*. Under this intricate proposal, foreign children born in Germany, providing one parent was born in Germany and if both parents had at least ten years' residence, could, upon application before the age of twelve, obtain a legal status equal to German children, but without full citizenship. This *Kinderstaatszugehörigkeit* would be converted into full nationality if the foreigner obtained release from his/her previous citizenship within one year of reaching the age of eighteen.

This proposal quickly came to be trivialised in the press as 'citizenship on a try-it-and-see basis' (*Schnupperstaatsbürgerschaft*), which respected legal commentators such as Kay Hailbronner judged to contain serious flaws (*Der Spiegel*, 22 April 1996). Apart from the fact that relatively few foreigners seeking naturalisation actually managed to be released from their previous citizenship in the space of twelve months, it raised issues of the holder's status in international law (for instance, regarding visa requirements). Furthermore, it failed to address one of the central flaws of the *Ausländergesetz*: that foreign children born in Germany could not join the German citizenry until their formative years were almost over. With even leading government figures admitting that these proposals were clumsy, the stage was set for the search for a politically acceptable alternative to become one of the most intractable problems of German domestic politics in the mid-1990s.

Just as during the reform of the *Ausländergesetz* in 1989 and 1990, the vast majority of the efforts to find a solution capable of building a majority were focused on the federal coalition. The attempts to revisit the issue were to lay bare the degree of polarisation the issue provoked within the coalition and especially within individual parties. Once again, the CDU itself was torn, with some sections favouring a sweeping reform, and others insisting on the status quo. In contrast to the *Ausländergesetz*, however, the conservative forces were not seeking a tightening of existing legislation. A consensus over the need to revise the RuStAG existed between all major parties, covering both government and opposition. Only when it came to the question of how large the step forward should be did opinions begin to diverge substantially.

The debate began as early as the summer of 1995, when it dawned on the FDP that it had miscalculated in agreeing to the *Kinderstaatszugehörigkeit*, in terms of both its practical implementation and of the party's own policy profile. Indeed, it remains a mystery why its chief negotiator, party leader Klaus Kinkel, ever consented to its inclusion in the coalition agreement. Certainly, the excuse of the then interior spokesman of the parliamentary party, Burkhard Hirsch, that the party feared that the formation of the entire coalition depended on this proposal, seems rather lame (*Der Spiegel*, 25 January 1999), given that the only mathematical alternative for the CDU/CSU would have been an unpalatable grand coalition with the SPD. What is certain is that the FDP beat a hasty retreat from this policy, and set about looking for alternatives (*Frankfurter Allgemeine Zeitung*, 16 September 1995).

Unfortunately, the CDU/CSU, and in particular the CSU, insisted on the *Kinderstaatszugehörigkeit* proposal. Having originally agreed to the proposal in the coalition negotiations, the FDP could do little to impose its own conceptions in the face of resolute opposition from the CDU/CSU. Its only hope, therefore, was that there would be a change of heart from within the senior coalition partner.

Debates within the CDU/CSU

Initially at least, its hopes were well founded. Over the years, a number of influential figures from within the CDU had expressed concern over the emphasis of *Ausländerpolitik* generally and citizenship policy more specifically, including Barbara John, the long-serving Commissioner for Foreigners' Affairs in Berlin, and Heiner Geißler, former CDU general secretary and cabinet minister (Geißler, 1982, 1991, 1993; John, 1987). The party's social-catholic wing, the *Christlich-Demokratische Arbeitnehmerschaft* (CDA), frequently served as a forum for such critical voices, and has itself been aware of the problems of children who are born as foreigners in Germany (cf. CDA, 1988). For many such children, the situation has been very difficult, being neither accepted as Germans because of their legal status as *Ausländer*, nor as nationals in their 'home' countries.

While such dissenters in the past were considered to be mavericks within the CDU, their cause did, in late 1995, gain momentum. Already, the widely respected former Federal President, Richard von Weizsäcker (CDU), had thrown his weight behind *ius soli* and dual citizenship (*Die Zeit*, 10 March 1995). Furthermore, on 6 October 1995, three younger

CDU members of the *Bundestag*, Peter Altmaier, Eckart von Klaeden and Norbert Röttgen, who were frustrated by the lack of progress since the coalition agreement of late 1994, published their own internal position paper for a new citizenship law. Confusingly called *Kinder-staatsANgehörigkeit*,[5] this envisaged giving full German citizenship to all children of non-national parents born in the Federal Republic, providing one parent was ordinarily resident there (i.e. *ius soli*). The proposal furthermore stipulated that beneficiaries of this model, who would normally also inherit their parents' citizenship(s) under *ius sanguinis*, would be required to settle on one citizenship upon reaching the age of twenty-one or twenty-three (the so-called *Optionsmodell*) (Altmaier, von Klaeden and Röttgen, 1995).

The paper also suggested a strict timetable for the reform to be completed by January 1998, in good time before the next federal election, and was notable for the importance it accorded the CDU/CSU *Fraktion*. Indeed, the Interior Ministry was not to be involved in formulating an offical bill until the parliamentary party had undertaken its own thorough negotiations on the issue. The idea that the Ministry, with all its technical expertise, should be presented with a *fait accompli*, in which all the major issues of substance had already been dealt with, speaks volumes on the frustration and mistrust it had engendered among moderate sections of the CDU. Simultaneously, the proposal potentially raised the profile and function of the parliamentary party, to the point at which it would effectively take the right of initiative from the executive.

This proposal received widespread coverage in the press, both because it publicised obvious differences within the CDU/CSU, but also because it went further than the SPD's own proposals for double *ius soli* (i.e. limited to third-generation foreigners). Initially, the paper was viewed benevolently by the leadership of the *Fraktion*, which set up a working party on citizenship policy. However, the months that followed saw little further progress: the three parliamentarians had powerful opponents, including Interior Minister Manfred Kanther, most sections of the CDU and the entire CSU. Their main criticism was that the proposal would create more dual citizens, at least in the first twenty-one years of the affected persons' lives. In reply, the proposal was launched in public in April 1996 (Altmaier, von Klaeden and Röttgen, 1996), followed up one month later by the publication of a list of 150 prominent CDU supporters, including no fewer than thirty-one members of the *Bundestag*. Yet in spite of such optimistic beginnings, including at least tacit support from Wolfgang Schäuble, the leader of the *Fraktion* (Interviews E and F), the proposal failed to move beyond the starting blocks. For the party leadership, the issue was simply too divisive (Interview F). With the majority of the CDU and the entire CSU standing its ground, the proposal was effectively killed off (*Frankfurter Allgemeine Zeitung*, 17 April 1996).

The final blow was struck on 10 and 11 November 1997, when the CDU's executive (*Vorstand*) followed by the combined CDU/CSU parliamentary party rejected the *Kinderstaatsangehörigkeit* proposal. In its place, the *Fraktion* adopted an amended version of the original *Kinderstaatszugehörigkeit* model. This new proposal aimed to give foreign children born in Germany a guarantee of naturalisation (*Einbürgerungszusicherung*) upon reaching the age of eighteen but with the prerequisite of good conduct and, of course, the renunciation of the applicant's previous citizenship.

It remains a moot point whether this revised version of the coalition agreement was ever likely to find its way onto the statute books. Most immediately, there was the spectre of difficult negotiations to secure the support of the junior coalition partner, the FDP. It had eagerly embraced the *Optionsmodell* (cf. Gerhardt, 1997: 109), which it continued to endorse up to and beyond the 1998 *Bundestag* election. However, apart from repeated futile public appeals to the CDU/CSU to reconsider its opposition to *ius soli*, it could do very little. Second, the *Bundesrat*, whose approval would be required, was at the time dominated by the SPD, which was already using its majority with great effect to harry the government's legislative agenda in other areas, especially tax reform. Faced with such hurdles, the 'naturalisation guarantee' stood little realistic chance of success, and with less than twelve months to go before the next *Bundestag* election, a non-decision was simply the easiest option. Schäuble himself admitted as much: 'All attempts to reach a tenable compromise for all the CDU/CSU and FDP's parliamentarians, which was necessary because of our limited majority in the *Bundestag* and because of the opposition's refusal to help us find a solution, failed. So we just decided not to bother' (Schäuble, 2001: 81). Meanwhile, the positions of the SPD and Greens on citizenship were growing ever closer. After years of opposition, during which the SPD had become progressively more liberal compared to its previous period in office and the Greens progressively less radical (cf. Murray, 1994), a more-or-less joint position had emerged by the mid-1990s (Bundestagsdrucksachen 13/423, 13/465). Both parties proposed a sweeping reduction in waiting times for naturalisation, the acceptance of dual citizenships, as well as the introduction of *ius soli*, although they differed over whether it should operate from the second or third generation.[6] As a result of this general convergence of ideas, the SPD and Greens were able to put forward a broadly united front during the no fewer than five occasions that the *Bundestag* debated citizenship, in addition to five further debates over *Ausländerpolitik* more generally, between 1994 and 1998.

In short, with widely differing party positions between government and opposition, as well as within the incumbent coalition and within the CDU, the reform of citizenship law was gridlocked and action restricted to faithfully repeated, but ultimately empty, statements of intent. It thus proved impossible to build a political majority for a new law by the time of the federal election on 27 September 1998.

The SPD–Green government's battles with citizenship reform, 1998–99

The defeat of Chancellor Helmut Kohl at the 1998 federal election constitutes a watershed moment in post-1945 German political history (Green, 1999). Not only did it end the longest chancellorship in the history of the Federal Republic, with the CDU/CSU polling its worst result since 1949, but it also represented the first full change in government brought about by the electorate; previously, all changes had involved one of the two members of the governing coalition seeking a new partner, thereby contributing to the sense of policy continuity identified by Katzenstein (1987). As a result, the first-ever SPD–Green government, led by Gerhard Schröder, took office on 27 October 1998.

Negotiating a new law

Throughout the 1998 election campaign, the SPD had stressed its desire for policy continuity. An SPD-led government was to be trusted to continue with the broad elements of public policy, rather than undertake a full reorientation of aims and contents. Schröder himself was memorably quoted as saying, 'we won't be doing everything differently, but we will be doing many things better'.

Citizenship, by contrast, was one policy area where the new government did plan to make a difference. In terms of policy priorities, this was an obvious choice, given that both the SPD and Greens had developed broadly similar positions during their time in opposition. As well as the strong symbolism of reforming a law which still dated back to the 'bad old days' of overt German ethnonationalism, something which was always going to go down well with the government's left-wing supporters, a reform had the added attraction of incurring relatively little financial cost. At the same time, many refugee groups, who by nature were relatively close to the Greens, were hoping for more liberal changes to other areas of *Ausländerpolitik*, and particularly in asylum policy (Prantl, 1999: 121).

Many of these hopes for a wider reform of *Ausländerpolitik* were to be dashed during the course of the coalition negotiations, which lasted throughout the first half of October 1998. The Greens' negotiators, Renate Künast and Kerstin Müller, were faced by Otto Schily and Herta Däubler-Gmelin, the designated SPD Interior and Justice Ministers, respectively. Schily, a former lawyer who had defended several members of the 1970s left-wing terrorist group, the Red Army Faction (RAF), had been one of the founding members of the Greens in the late 1970s. But he had left the party under a cloud to join the SPD in 1989 and proceeded there to reinvent himself as a self-confessed law-and-order man.

Because of his history, there was a lively mutual antipathy between Schily and his counterparts from the Greens. The negotiations were thus punctuated by some colourful clashes of personalities, which in themselves affected the outcome of the coalition negotiations. For instance, Schily deliberately riled the Greens by refusing point-blank to consider their proposals for a full-scale immigration law, or a liberalisation of asylum policy (*Süddeutsche Zeitung*, 15 October 1998). Consequently, in asylum and immigration policy the final coalition agreement limited itself to a promise to review the 'fast-track' decision procedure at airports which had been introduced as part of the 1993 asylum reforms. The two parties did also agree to introduce Germany's first self-contained anti-discrimination law, a decision which in turn facilitated the agreement of two directives in the EU's Council of Ministers in 2000 (cf. p. 16). However, despite the Justice Ministry issuing a draft bill in December 2001, widespread criticism from societal organisations mean that it proved impossible to complete this project by the time of the 2002 federal election.

In citizenship policy, the negotiations were relatively straightforward, albeit not without one major row. The SPD negotiators did accede quickly to the Greens' desire that the new law should include a general tolerance of multiple citizenships. This not only constituted a potentially groundbreaking departure from existing policy but was also to have far-reaching consequences for policy three months down the line. But it was the question of *ius soli* which produced one of the biggest disagreements of the entire negotiations, which was finally resolved only after intervention by the leadership of both parties (*Süddeutsche Zeitung*, 16 October 1998; Hurrelmann, 2001: 253). The sticking point was whether citizenship via *ius soli* should be limited to the third generation (so-called double *ius soli*), which represented the SPD's position, or whether it should be available from the second generation (so-called simple *ius soli*), which was the Greens' position. Schily absolutely insisted that double *ius soli* was necessary to guarantee that the beneficiaries were properly integrated. In a typical example of how political negotiations can work, a compromise was suggested that double *ius soli* should be supplemented by simple *ius soli* for children of non-nationals who had immigrated during childhood. When asked by Kerstin Müller to suggest an age limit, Schily picked out fourteen almost at random, and the deal was done (Interview C).

The CDU/CSU mobilises against dual citizenship

So it was that the coalition agreement contained a proposal for nothing less than a whole-scale reform of Germany's nationality provisions. With its general acceptance of dual citizenships and the introduction of *ius soli* for the first time in the history of German nationality law, the government's plans promised to fundamentally alter the basis on which Germany's citizenry was defined. In its aims, the government was emboldened by its strong position in the *Bundesrat*, in which its blocking majority from the Kohl era had now become an enabling mechanism. Indeed, for the first time since the early 1990s, the two chambers of parliament had similar political majorities. Although an election was due in the state of Hesse on 7 February 1999, a defeat for its incumbent SPD–Green coalition seemed unthinkable: the *Land* had been solidly SPD ever since 1945, with only one short CDU interlude in the late 1980s.

However, the issue of dual citizenship was soon to emerge as the Achilles' heel of the government's plans. In his memoirs, Wolfgang Schäuble, who by now had replaced Helmut Kohl as CDU party leader, writes of his fear that a government bill based on the *Optionsmodell*

would split both the opposition and the CDU, and of his subsequent
relief that the government intended to accept dual citizenship as a matter
of course, which gave him a focal point to rally both the CDU and CSU
around (Schäuble, 2001: 81–2). With the new government announcing
in November 1998, soon after taking power, that citizenship reform
would top its legislative agenda, the CDU/CSU was therefore presented
with a golden opportunity to regroup politically following its heavy
defeat at the 1998 election. It was well aware that the public as a
whole remained deeply sceptical about dual citizenship, and it sought
to tap into this by launching its now infamous petition campaign
(*Unterschriftenaktion*) against this element of the reform.

In the run-up to Christmas 1998, the idea of launching such a
campaign had been discussed by Schäuble and the new leader of the
CSU, Edmund Stoiber. With no other veto points available to the
opposition, a legally non-binding petition campaign seemed an ideal,
if unconventional method of mobilising the population against the
government's plans (Cooper, 2002). The idea was enthusiastically en-
dorsed by the CDU's candidate in the upcoming Hesse election, Roland
Koch, who understandably saw this as a perfect opportunity to galvanise
an otherwise tepid election campaign. But there was a bigger prize at
stake, too. If the CDU and FDP were to win the state of Hesse, the
SPD–Green absolute majority in the *Bundesrat* would be lost. Without
this absolute majority, the new citizenship bill could not be passed, and
a compromise with the opposition parties would have to be sought.
Therefore, on 4 January 1999, even before Interior Minister Schily had
actually published his citizenship bill, Schäuble and Stoiber launched
their campaign. Stoiber, who had a well-earned reputation for polemi-
cising, taunted the Greens by suggesting that multiple citizenships
threatened the existence of the German state in the same way that the
left-wing RAF terrorists had done in the 1970s and 1980s.

Meanwhile, the deputy CDU leader, Jürgen Rüttgers, was hastily
charged with developing a *post hoc* integration and citizenship strategy
around which the party could unite against the government. This proved
to be a delicate task. With a substantial minority of the CDU still
preferring the *Optionsmodell*, which would have involved at least the
temporary toleration of dual citizenships, and with the CSU absolutely
refusing to support this, Rüttgers was left with no option but to fall
back onto the 'naturalisation guarantee' model which had been agreed,
but never implemented, two years earlier (*Süddeutsche Zeitung*, 14
January 1999). In consequence, the CDU/CSU's parliamentary bill on

citizenship (Bundestagsdrucksache 14/535) neither included *ius soli* nor made any provision for dual citizenship beyond the existing regulations. Ultimately, the liberal elements once again acquiesced to the majority opinion in the interests of party unity, but only after around fifty members (or one-fifth) of the parliamentary party, including senior figures such as the CDU general secretary Angela Merkel, had voted in favour of the *Optionsmodell* at a meeting on 19 January 1999 (*Frankfurter Rundschau*, 21 January 1999). Nor was the petition campaign universally accepted within the CDU: many key figures were highly critical of such an overtly polarising tactic, and the Saarland party refused to participate (*Frankfurter Rundschau*, 3 February 1999). Only the CSU stood united, in both its opposition to dual citizenship and in its support of the petition campaign. Yet despite intense criticism from churches, unions and liberal commentators alike, the CDU/CSU leadership was clearly willing to risk promoting anti-foreigner resentments in the interests of wrecking the government's plans. As Schäuble himself notes:

> During an interview with two journalists from [the highly respected liberal weekly newspaper – SG] *Die Zeit* … I realised how difficult it would be to defuse allegations of anti-foreigner populism. Nonetheless, I was more determined than ever to push ahead with the petition campaign. (Schäuble, 2001: 86)

In fact, the government had been completely caught out by the CDU/CSU's blatantly populist offensive. Instead of meeting the opposition's rhetoric head on, the SPD and especially the Greens were reduced to expressing their outrage at the CDU's poor political manners (Hurrelmann, 2001). At the same time, Interior Minister Schily once again outmanoeuvred the Greens by introducing some decidedly conservative markers into the bill, which was drafted by the Interior Ministry and presented on 13 January 1999. Although it formally corresponded to the contents of the coalition treaty, the small print quickly revealed that the requirements for naturalisation were actually tightened in several areas: in contrast to the existing simplified naturalisation procedure, the new bill excluded foreigners on social security and unemployment benefit from naturalisation, as well as requiring applicants both to possess adequate language skills and to declare their loyalty to the constitution. Moreover, the bill standardised the level of fees payable at DM 500, which represented a five-fold increase over the reduced level for 'simplified naturalisations' under the *Ausländergesetz* (cf. Table 4.1).

Table 4.1 Summary of citizenship reform proposals, 1998–99

	Policy in 1999	1st government proposal (pre-Hesse)	2nd government proposal (post-Hesse)
Standard discretionary naturalisation	Minimum 10 years' residence	Minimum 5 years' residence	No change from 1999 policy
Simplified naturalisation for young foreigners	Legal right between ages 16 and 23, with 8 years' residence and 6 years in German school	Legal right after 5 years' residence	No specific provisions
Simplified naturalisation for other foreigners	Legal right after 15 years' residence	Legal right after 8 years' residence	Legal right after 8 years' residence
Principal exclusions	Criminal record, drawing of unemployment benefit or income support (with exceptions for hardship); NB *not* absence of language skills	Criminal record, drawing of unemployment benefit or income support, anti-constitutional activities, absence of language skills	Criminal record, drawing of unemployment benefit or income support (with exceptions for hardship), anti-constitutional activities, absence of language skills
Ius soli	No	Yes, if one parent born in Germany or immigrated before age 14	Yes, from second generation if one parent has 8 years' residence and secure residence permit; also 12-month transition arrangements for children born after 1 January 1990
Dual citizenship	No, except if home state did not normally release its citizens or failed to do so within reasonable time limit; toleration also possible if release made dependent on performing national service	Yes	No change from 1999 policy, but with more exceptions. Also via *ius soli* to age 23, at which time German citizenship is revoked unless release from other citizenship can be proven
Naturalisation fees	DM 100 (simplified)/DM 500 (standard)	No change from 1999 policy	DM 500

While the Greens were certainly annoyed at this, their attention was quickly diverted to the CDU/CSU's petition campaign, which got under way in Hesse just four days later on 17 January 1999. Its resonance with the voting public was immediate and undeniable, with the stalls in Frankfurt attracting up to 500 signatories an hour. On 23 January 1999, the campaign was extended across Germany, amid the predictable mix of localised scuffles and individual (mainly elderly) members of the public asking where they could 'sign up against foreigners' (quoted in Schäuble, 2001: 88; see also *Süddeutsche Zeitung*, 25 January 1999). Nonetheless, the campaign was extraordinarily successful, and by May 1999, the two parties claimed to have collected some 5 million signatures (*Frankfurter Rundschau*, 21 May 1999).

The campaign thus confirmed what opinion polls had shown for many years, namely that voters were overwhelmingly sceptical of the proposed introduction of dual citizenships as a rule. What is more, this scepticism ran through almost all the main parties' electorates, with only the Greens' voters clearly in favour (Table 4.2).

Table 4.2 Public opinion on dual citizenship, 1999

	January 1999		February 1999	
	For (%)	*Against* (%)	*For* (%)	*Against* (%)
Total	32	63	27	68
SPD voters	44	50	37	59
CDU/CSU voters	15	81	12	82
Green voters	70	30	69	28
FDP voters	26	59	30	67
PDS voters	45	52	44	52

Source: *Politbarometer* polls, January and February 1999 (Forschungsgruppe Wahlen, 2000). 'Don't knows' account for the remainder.

In the context of the all-important Hesse election on 7 February 1999, the petition campaign was supported by two-thirds of CDU voters, which proved to be decisive in terms of voter mobilisation. The CDU clearly emerged as the victor, and Koch was able to form a coalition with the FDP. Tellingly, it was the Greens who effectively lost the election for the government, by losing four percentage points; the SPD actually marginally increased its vote share. Post-election analyses showed that while dual citizenship had not been the deciding issue in the election, it had certainly been instrumental in encouraging traditional CDU voters to turn out (Schmitt-Beck, 2000).

As a result, the SPD–Green government now lacked the necessary *Bundesrat* majority to push its citizenship bill through parliament. Although the leadership of the Greens initially urged the SPD to stand firm, Oskar Lafontaine, the SPD leader, quickly indicated his party's intention to amend the original proposal (*Die Welt*, 10 February 1999), with the aim of bringing the opposition FDP on board. Its coalition with the SPD in the state of Rhineland-Palatinate wielded enough votes in the *Bundesrat* to reinstate the government's majority, thereby avoiding the need to negotiate directly with the CDU/CSU on this matter, a prospect which many party activists found galling in the light of the petition campaign. Following these negotiations, a new bill was presented which both removed the general acceptance of dual citizenship from the bill, and also introduced, at the behest of the FDP, simple *ius soli*. In addition, the revised bill envisaged that any dual citizens thereby created would lose their German nationality by the age of twenty-three unless they secured release from their other citizenship (see Table 4.1 above; also Green, 2000). The Greens fought a rearguard action by attempting to retain general dual citizenship for the over-sixties, but when the FDP rejected this, the party was forced to content itself with the reinstatement of a hardship clause for unemployed naturalisation applicants, as well as bringing in the now automatic acceptance of dual citizenship for applications by recognised refugees. Once again, the Greens were successfully sidelined by the SPD, as Hurrelmann notes (2001: 259–61): the party was actually excluded from the crucial final meeting in Mainz on 11 March 1999, when Interior Minister Schily closed the deal with the FDP.

Compared to the emotionally charged events of the petition campaign, the bill's passage through parliament was relatively straightforward. The government adopted many of the parliamentary tactics employed by the CDU/CSU–FDP government in 1990 to push the *Ausländergesetz* through the *Bundestag* (see Chapter 3), and the opposition CDU/CSU predictably railed against what it saw as the undue haste the government was displaying in this matter. A detailed hearing was held by the Interior Affairs Select Committee on 13 April 1999, the composition of which, as on previous occasions, spoke volumes about the level at which the discourse over citizenship reform was located: of the fourteen experts whose evidence was invited, nine were academics and only one represented the views of the immigrant community (Deutscher Bundestag Innenausschuss, 1999). The sense of a cross-party charade was confirmed by the committee's recommendations, in which

the opposition's suggestions and concerns were again summarily ignored by the governing parties (Bundestagsdrucksache 14/867). The
plenary debates on 19 March and 7 May 1999 were polarised and at
times heated (Deutscher Bundestag Plenarprotokoll 14/28 and 14/40),
with the government breaking with parliamentary tradition by schedul-
ing the joint second and third readings during the week normally
reserved for the budget debate (Deutscher Bundestag Plenarprotokoll
14/37). There was also a final sting in the tail for the CDU/CSU
leadership in the *Bundestag*, as no fewer than twenty-three of its members, including most of the moderate wing, abstained from the final
vote on the third reading, rather than voting against the bill. With the
temporary government majority in the *Bundesrat* ensuring that the bill's
final legislative hurdle was taken on 21 May 1999, the new, reformed
citizenship law came into force on 1 January 2000.

Semisovereignty and citizenship reform in Germany

Despite being hailed as a historic innovation by several speakers during
the parliamentary debates in March and May 1999, the new citizenship
law's provenance as a messy political compromise, first between the
SPD and Greens and later with the FDP joining in, cannot be disguised.
Certainly, the introduction of *ius soli* and the (at least temporary)
toleration of dual citizenship does mark a turning point in German
citizenship law. But a number of serious technical and legal deficits with
this provision have since become apparent (cf. *Der Spiegel*, 5 April 1999;
Green, 2000; Dornis, 2002: 171–3; Göbel-Zimmermann, 2003). For
instance, children qualify for German nationality via *ius soli* only if one
parent has lived in Germany for at least eight years *and* has the
corresponding residence permit to match. As the Appendix indicates
(although a precise figure is difficult to calculate here), the proportion
of non-nationals with the minimum residence period is considerably
higher than that with the necessary residence permit. The result of this
double requirement is that only between 40 and 50 per cent of children
born to foreign parents in Germany actually qualify for the *ius soli*
provision. In addition, because children from former guestworker countries could live in Germany without a residence permit prior to 1997,
their residence period, both for the purposes of naturalisation and for
ius soli for their children, can be documented only from this year
onwards. Most importantly, the issue of the German state actually

withdrawing its nationality gained via *ius soli* once the beneficiary reaches the age of twenty-three remains constitutionally highly disputed, and is certain to end up before the Constitutional Court soon after 2013.[7]

What is also interesting about the focus on dual citizenship during the public and political debates of 1998 and 1999 is that it epitomises the location of policy discourse at the symbolic, rather than the practical level. Hagedorn (2001: 173–218) shows clearly that abstract terms such as 'loyalty', 'integration', 'value of citizenship' and 'national identity' played a central role in policy discourses of the late 1990s, not only in Germany but also in France. Indeed, one of the main arguments brought by the CDU/CSU during the petition campaign against dual citizenship was that the 'exit option' of having a second passport provided no incentive to show loyalty and commitment to Germany, and was therefore actually counterproductive in terms of integration. This question will be explored in more detail in Chapter 5.

Although this dispute has been no less intense for its symbolic nature, it quite simply ignored the reality of dual citizenship in Germany. As Chapter 2 has pointed out, Germany's rejection of dual citizenship has always been qualified by a number of exceptions (see Table 4.1), which were actually extended in the new citizenship law. Thus, whereas the proportion of naturalisations tolerating dual citizenship fluctuated between 20 and 38 per cent during the 1990s, this had shot up to almost 50 per cent in 2001 (see the Appendix). When added to the descendants of bi-national parents, who are routinely dual nationals under *ius sanguinis*, the number of dual citizens in Germany is conventionally estimated to be at least 2 million (see breakdown in Bundestagsdrucksache 14/509: 6–10).

At the same time, Germany for decades itself contributed to the proliferation of dual citizenship abroad. Under the RuStAG's unlimited provision for *ius sanguinis*, German citizenship, providing the holder had not naturalised elsewhere, could be passed on abroad to descendants for generations to come. But the most crass example of Germany's double standards with dual citizenship is ethnic German immigrants, who have never been required to give up their Polish, Kazakhi or Russian citizenship: this was considered to be an 'unreasonable hardship' (*unzumutbare Härte*) for this already privileged group.

Crucially, despite dual citizenship being implemented more generously than in the past, the outcome of the 1999 citizenship law, if defined as its actual impact on naturalisation numbers, is once again clearly incremental (cf. Green, 2000: 113–14). As the Appendix shows, the number of naturalisations did rise sharply in 2000, principally as a result of the transitional arrangements for children born between 1990 and 2000 (see Table 4.1). However, since then, the number has fallen two years in a row, to the extent that the level in 2002 was only 12,000, or some 8 per cent, higher than that achieved in 1999 under the old system of simplified naturalisation. It is certainly true that over half of the 1.3 million persons who became German citizens between 1980 and 2002 did so in the last five years of that period. But in terms of increasing this trajectory in order to make real progress towards the 1984 goal of greater inclusion of non-nationals (see Chapter 3), the new law's impact to the end of the period under consideration here has been disappointing. As noted in the introduction to this chapter, the number of non-nationals in Germany remained static at 7.3 million between 1998 and 2002; a successful citizenship policy would have started to bring about a gradual reduction in this number, by making citizenship the next logical step for long-term resident non-nationals.

To a lesser extent, the epithet of incrementalism even applies to the immigration and asylum reform of 1993. Although the numbers of new asylum seekers did fall dramatically in 1993 and 1994, it was to be another five years before they dropped below 100,000; in 2002, they still remained above the average level for the 1980s. It must also be noted that the reduction in applications has not encouraged Germany, which has always taken a comparatively restrictive line on grounds for recognition, to be more generous in granting asylum: initial recognition rates have rarely risen above 12 per cent annually, and in 2002, just 5 per cent of applications were accepted (see Appendix).[8]

An even more gradualist solution is represented by the deal on ethnic Germans, whose immigration is set to fade away only over the next decades, rather than the next years (Münz and Ulrich, 1999: 26). The continuing potential for immigration via this source is illustrated by the fact that in 2001, under 25 per cent of *Spätaussiedler* were actually ethnic Germans: the remaining 75 per cent were dependants and descendants who enjoyed the same rights to citizenship and social benefits regardless of their ethnic origin (*Der Spiegel*, 24 February 2003). What is more, with around 70 per cent of ethnic Germans voting for the CDU/CSU (Wüst, 2002), there is little political incentive for this policy actor to help curtail their immigration further.

How, then, can the policy-making process and semisovereign governance help account for both the timing and outcome of the citizenship law? In terms of timing, given that a reform of citizenship was at least politically inconceivable prior to unification, the focus must be on the 1990s. Here, the CDU/CSU's preference for a non-decision, and its ability to implement it, was the first absolutely critical factor, especially between 1994 and 1998. The extent of the ideological distance between the parties meant that the CDU/CSU, as the actor whose position was closest to the status quo, stood to lose the most from any reform. For it, a non-decision was therefore the ideal solution. In effect, it was also an acceptable outcome for the FDP, which was clearly unwilling to risk bringing down the government over an issue such as citizenship. Ironically, a compromise constructed around the *Optionsmodell*, which had been invented by CDU politicians and which represented the median position among the various proposals, would easily have found a parliamentary majority (*Die Zeit*, 16 February 1996). It is all the more ironic that this idea was hijacked, first by the FDP and later by the SPD, to form the centrepiece of the new law.

In reality, it is not at all certain whether more progress would have been made if the Kohl government had been re-elected in 1998, given the previously irreconcilable nature of the differences between CDU/CSU and the FDP. In terms of timing, the historic change of government in 1998 was therefore the second vital ingredient for policy change, as it removed the principal veto player (the CDU/CSU) from power at the federal level and simultaneously replaced the moderate FDP with the more radical Greens as the junior coalition partner.

The change of government also had a critical effect on outcomes. The coalition negotiations included the remarkably bold decision to introduce a wholesale liberalisation of dual citizenship, which unfortunately turned out to be one of the biggest miscalculations in recent German political history. The implications of this decision have been huge: apart from leading to an ultimately much more modest reform, which was a considerable disappointment to the government's core supporters, it also cost the new government its precious, and unique, *Bundesrat* majority. From the 1999 Hesse election onwards, the SPD–Green government was faced with the same constraints as the Kohl government had been from 1991 to 1998.

Once again, the main elements of semisovereignty can be clearly identified in the reform process. Coalition politics enabled the FDP to stop the original *Kinderstaatszugehörigkeit* model from ever becoming law; equally, they also allowed the CDU/CSU to prevent the *Optionsmodell* from being adopted. In making its non-decision, the

Ressortprinzip of ministerial autonomy was a crucial resource for the CDU/CSU: its Interior Minister, Manfred Kanther, could simply refuse to draft a bill.

In addition, federalism played a particularly important role in determining policy outcome. The defeat of the SPD–Green coalition in Hesse tipped the balance in the *Bundesrat* in favour of the opposition, although it was still possible to circumvent the CDU/CSU by negotiating with the FDP. Had this failed, the CDU/CSU's ability to influence or block the bill would have been even stronger. Nonetheless, the citizenship bill underlines just how powerful a veto point the *Bundesrat* can be in consent laws, which require an absolute majority of votes. It is worth remembering that the SPD and Greens were forced to deal with the FDP despite being by far the largest bloc in the *Bundesrat*, with thirty out of sixty-nine votes even after the Hesse election.

The effects of cooperative federalism are clearly visible, too. Even though the necessary secondary legislation law was passed relatively quickly in 2000, substantial regional variations in naturalisation persist (Dornis, 2002: 169). One important factor behind such variations is that the secondary legislation allowed the *Länder* considerable leeway in deciding how to interpret the requirement for 'adequate' language skills and also whether to confirm the constitutional loyalty of applicants with the domestic intelligence service. Predictably, such criteria are interpreted more stringently by some states (including Bavaria) than by others, but the net effect has been a very uneven pattern of implementation (Göbel-Zimmermann, 2003: 73–4).

Above all, and just like during the formulation of the *Ausländergesetz*, the development of *Ausländerpolitik* during the 1990s underlines the pivotal role of the coalition parties. Not only did the three main political parties hammer out the asylum compromise among themselves, but the debates over *ius soli* between 1994 and 1998 took place almost entirely within the CDU/CSU parliamentary party; indeed, it was in the *Fraktion* that the deciding vote over the 'naturalisation guarantee' proposal was taken in 1997. This pattern continued after the change of government in 1998, although the Interior Ministry did regain some of its influence, largely as a result of Interior Minister Schily's high profile within government. But it was still the parties which were the main protagonists at every stage of the reform process and most obviously in the CDU/CSU's decision to proceed with the petition campaign. In this respect, the absence both of major societal players and of parapublic institutions from the constellation of decision-making policy actors was significant. It meant that there was no non-political constraint on the CDU/CSU's decision to use such an undoubtedly populist, and arguably high-risk, tactic in order to bring about policy change.

The citizenship case study also highlights two less obvious aspects of the semisovereignty model. First, despite the federal government's semi-sovereignty in its ability to dictate policy, it remains *primus inter pares* among policy actors. The problem in citizenship policy between 1990 and 1998 was not that the government's initiatives were blocked by an opposition-dominated *Bundesrat*, but rather that the government did not make any initiatives which could be blocked. In contrast to other issues such as tax reform, the government was not willing to test the resolve of the SPD–Green majority in the *Bundesrat* to hold out against its proposals. The CDU/CSU–FDP coalition evidently judged that the nature of the issue meant either that individual SPD-states would not be susceptible to 'side payments', or that citizenship rights for foreigners were simply not worth the political and financial capital necessary to win over the *Bundesrat*. Either way, a non-decision was again the logical outcome. The case study thereby demonstrates that while other actors can veto proposals, it is only the federal government who can push through a non-decision.

Second, the events highlight the significance of the coalition agreement. The evidence from both the post-1994 and the post-1998 coalition negotiations shows how easily compromises can be made which only subsequently turn out to be far from perfect. Even though it was already clear by late 1995 that the *Kinderstaatszugehörigkeit* proposal was unfeasible, the fact that it was contained in the coalition agreement meant that all partners had to agree to change it, which at least the CSU refused to do. This effectively gave one of the junior coalition partners an incredibly powerful veto position over government policy. If citizenship policy had not been specifically covered in the coalition agreement, the FDP might perhaps even have been more tempted to vote with the opposition's bills, as this would not have constituted a technical breach of this agreement.

Lastly, this case study once again illustrates the power of path dependency in Germany, in both the long and short term. From a long-term perspective, radical and sudden departures from existing practices, such as the government's plan to end the rejection of dual citizenship, can invariably be defeated, even if the methods chosen are relatively unconventional. But in the short term, too, coalition agreements can entail path dependency, albeit in a more limited form. The aftermath of the coalition agreements in 1994 and 1998 shows very clearly that coalition partners should always look before they leap.

Notes

1 As *ius soli* ascribes citizenship at birth, it is not technically a naturalisation and is therefore not usually recorded separately.
2 The use of *ius soli* normally creates dual citizenships for children born of non-national parents, as they usually also inherit their parents' citizenship(s) via *ius sanguinis*.
3 In addition, dual citizenship could (but did not have to) be tolerated if the applicant was required to perform military service before being released from his/her citizenship.
4 Despite its temporary nature, the *Duldung* is surprisingly common: in 2000, over around 260,000 persons resided in Germany on its basis. Moreover, 25 per cent of these permits had first been issued in 1997 or earlier. For this reason, this status has been heavily criticised by refugee groups.
5 Author's emphasis: the semantic difference between *Kinderstaatszu-* and *Kinderstaatsangehörigkeit* is impossible to translate, as the former represents an artificial linguistic construct.
6 The SPD's proposal was also more detailed in that it considered other important issues such as the conditions under which German citizenship would be lost.
7 The first cases will already arise around 2013 because of the twelve-month transition arrangement in the law which granted German citizenship via *ius soli* to any child reaching the age of ten in 2000 if one parent fulfilled the new criteria at the time of the child's birth. The first members of this group will reach the age of majority in 2008, and could therefore potentially lose their German nationality in 2013.
8 However, the final recognition rate usually increases once successful appeals are added.

5

Immigration, integration and the negotiation of the *Zuwanderungsgesetz*, 2000–2

The coming into force of Germany's new citizenship regime on 1 January 2000 marks the end of a particularly controversial episode in the history of *Ausländerpolitik*. The whole affair had sent the government reeling and left its core voters disillusioned (Prantl, 1999; Lees, 2000), and both coalition partners suffered heavy defeats at the five *Land* elections held during the autumn of 1999. But there was to be little respite for the government, as a debate about a full-scale immigration law (*Zuwanderungsgesetz*) exploded onto the political agenda in 2000 and 2001.[1]

The fact that a German government was even considering such a law represented a remarkable shift in elite opinion. As the previous chapters have shown, the notion that Germany was 'not a country of immigration' had guided most policy decisions throughout the previous decades and was in fact the consensus position during the 1960s and 1970s. In the 1980s and 1990s, this increasingly became limited to the CDU/CSU, which was however able to prevent any departure from this principle due to its dominant position as the largest party of government. For instance, Interior Minister Manfred Kanther in 1995 again rejected opposition calls for an active management of immigration with the argument that, as Germany evidently did not need new immigration, what was there to manage (*Die Welt*, 28 April 1995)? Nonetheless, during the coalition negotiations following the 1998 election, which brought the somewhat more liberal SPD and the much more liberal Greens into government, the new SPD Interior Minister Otto Schily also refused to accept Green demands for such a law (see Chapter 4). Shortly afterwards, Schily, perhaps even intentionally, provoked outrage among the Greens by declaring that 'Germany's capacity for immigration has been exceeded' (*Der Spiegel*, 30 November 1998). As the liberal commentator Heribert Prantl noted (1999: 126), this statement revealed that Schily was just as capable of tarring all foreigners with the same brush as his more conservative predecessors had done.

Yet within just two years, Schily himself was presenting a bill for the *Zuwanderungsgesetz*. In its scope, this bill was groundbreaking: it was to regulate new, high-skilled labour migration, introduce new formal integration courses for non-nationals, improve the situation for refugees and provide a simplification of Germany's complex residence policy.[2] In short, the bill fundamentally challenged the orthodoxy in a whole range of issues in *Ausländerpolitik* and thereby represented a potentially path defining moment.

The negotiation of this law and its legislation under controversial circumstances in the *Bundesrat* on 22 March 2002 constitutes this book's final case study. As was the case with previous chapters, the process of policy formulation reveals the key characteristics of the semisovereign state, in terms of both actors and outcomes. In addition, path dependency and the tendency towards symbolic politics are also clearly visible.

Why, though, did it come to this remarkable development? Two main reasons can be identified: the perceived need for new labour migration and issues of integration.

Labour migration returns to the political agenda

The first factor behind the political pressure for a self-contained immigration law was a surge in calls for Germany to permit new full-time labour migration for the first time since the 1973 *Anwerbestopp*. Already in December 1990, the federal government had issued two regulations (*Verordnungen*) to permit seasonal and other temporary labour migration, for instance in agriculture, and a total of over 1.3 million such work permits were issued in 1995. However, as the introduction to Chapter 1 has already noted, two new problems created pressure for a more comprehensive liberalisation: the impact of long-term demographic developments and increasing evidence of the existence of skills shortages.

The 'Green Card' programme

By 2000, widespread skills shortages were being reported in a number of sectors of the economy. These included both high-skilled and lower-skilled professions, such as engineering and the hotels and restaurant trade, as well as strategic growth areas such as information technology

(IT) and biotechnology. Indeed, in IT alone, industry representatives estimated that some 150,000 vacancies needed to be filled in the medium term (*Die Welt*, 23 February 2001). Despite around 3.7 million registered unemployed in Germany in early 2000, these vacancies could not be filled, and industry representatives began to lobby the government intensely to allow firms to recruit from abroad. On 23 February 2000, at the annual Cebit Computer Fair in Hanover, Chancellor Schröder responded by announcing plans for what came to be known as the 'Green Card' programme. Under this label, industry would be allowed to hire up to 20,000 IT specialists from outside the EU for up to five years each, providing that the recipients were educated to degree level or earned a salary of over DM 100,000 p. a.[3] While the scheme included the possibility of dependant migration, it was clearly a short-term, highly specific measure, aimed at meeting shortages in the IT sector alone, which was moreover seen as strategically important to the then booming 'new economy'. Accordingly, calls by industry to extend this scheme to other sectors, including lower-skilled professions, were firmly rejected by the government, although it did shortly afterwards attempt to alleviate further labour market pressures by allowing asylum seekers to work following a one-year waiting period.

Despite being distinctly modest in its scope, the 'Green Card' initiative completely transformed the public debate over immigration. Suddenly, the issue was no longer whether Germany needed immigration, but how much it needed. This in turn made the issue of whether Germany was a country of immigration irrelevant: the fact was, it had to attract highly skilled immigrants to remain economically competitive. The debate also turned traditional lines of political conflict over immigration on their head: employers' organisations were now siding with the SPD-led government, while the unions, for whom the 'Green Card' smacked of new guestworker recruitment, found themselves initially aligned with the CDU/CSU, who questioned the wisdom of such proposals given high levels of unemployment in Germany, among both nationals and non-nationals.

In this potentially volatile environment, and with no parapublic institutions taking the heat out of the issue, it was the CDU's turn to make a political miscalculation over *Ausländerpolitik*. Following its triumph at the previous autumn's *Land* elections, the party had crashed back to earth as a result of the revelation that senior party figures, including Chancellor Kohl, had broken party finance laws over many years. The scandal had already cost the CDU victory at the Schleswig-Holstein election on 27 February 2000, and now threatened to scupper its chances at the even more important election in Germany's largest state, North Rhine-Westphalia, which was scheduled for 14 May 2000. The CDU's candidate there, Jürgen Rüttgers, who had in fact formulated the joint CDU/CSU position on citizenship during the petition campaign in early 1999, therefore went onto the offensive over immigration by coining the blatantly populist slogan 'Children, not Indians' (*Kinder statt Inder*). This alluded to the perception that Indian IT specialists would be targeted for the 'Green Card' and simultaneously brought across the CDU's argument that government policy should concentrate on educating Germany's children to fill skills shortages, rather than meet them through new immigration. As had been the case previously with so many other issues of *Ausländerpolitik*, this campaign tactic again split the CDU along familiar lines, as party moderates criticised what they saw to be a gross distortion of the immigration issue. More importantly, it failed to impress the voters: not only did the CDU fail to unseat the SPD in North Rhine-Westphalia, but the election actually saw a slight drop in the party's vote share.

The CDU's inability to mobilise its voters around immigration in the way it had managed to do so during the 1999 Hesse election with dual citizenship had an important impact on government thinking. Initially, the 'Green Card' proposal had been only cautiously welcomed within the SPD's parliamentary party. Throughout 2000 and 2001, opinion polls consistently confirmed that voters remained deeply suspicious of new immigration. With memories of the previous year's petition campaign still fresh, there was little appetite for yet another highly emotive and potentially damaging dispute over immigration. In addition, many in the SPD, including Labour Minister Walter Riester, shared the unions' and CDU/CSU's wariness over new labour migration in an era of already high unemployment, which moreover disproportionately affected non-nationals (see Appendix). However, Rüttgers' failure in North Rhine-Westphalia, combined with a rosier economic outlook and continued lobbying from industry encouraged Chancellor Schröder and Interior Minister Schily to revisit their initial rejection of an immigration law in 1998 in favour of regulating this issue before the 2002 *Bundestag* election (*Der Spiegel*, 12 June 2000).

Immigration and the demographic challenge

In this, they were encouraged by the re-emergence of a second development onto the public agenda: the long-term demographic implications

of Germany's ageing and shrinking population. As in other EU countries, life expectancy in Germany has risen steadily, and in 2000 stood
at seventy-five and eighty-one years for men and women, respectively.
Men who were aged sixty in 2000 could expect to live a further nineteen
years; for women, the corresponding figure was twenty-four years
(Schmid, 2001). Yet at the same time, Germany's fertility rate (defined
as the number of children born per woman) has fallen to among the
lowest in the EU, standing at just 1.3 in 1999; in the new *Länder*, it was
lower still at 0.8, well short of the level of 2.1 needed to maintain the
size of a country's population. In consequence, Germany's population
has been predicted to shrink from over 80 million to between 60 and
70 million by 2050 (Statistisches Bundesamt, 2000). As a result, the
combination of ever-more pensioners living ever longer, but ever-fewer
persons working to generate the taxes necessary to support their growing
demands for pensions and health care, threatens to plunge Germany's
social security and pensions systems into crisis at some stage during the
first half of the twenty-first century.

Of course, this development has not crept up overnight: the number
of deaths has been exceeding the number of live births in Germany ever
since the early 1970s, necessarily leading to a population decrease in
the long term. Katzenstein, too, had already underlined the fundamental
nature of the demographic challenge in the mid-1980s (Katzenstein,
1987: 191–2). Even Wolfgang Schäuble, then Minister of State at the
Federal Chancellery under Helmut Kohl, had written in an essay in
1988 that Germany would need more immigration to compensate for
population decline (quoted in Meier-Braun, 2002: 67). However, during
2000, the issue returned to the spotlight, helped by the publication
in March of a high-profile cross-national comparison of replacement
migration by the UN Population Division. This dramatically underlined
the extent of the challenge faced by Germany, by modelling the relationship between demographics, net immigration and a country's
potential support ratio (PSR), which measures the ratio of the number
of economically active people to those aged sixty-five and over (United
Nations, 2000). In its most optimistic of its realistic scenarios, which
assumed net annual migration to Germany of 200,000 persons, the
report predicted that the PSR would halve from its 1995 level of 4.4:1
to just 2.1:1 by 2050.

This realisation added extra weight to argument for new labour
migration. Certainly, measures such as longer working lives, lower
pension benefits and higher workforce participation rates of women

and older workers all had a role to play in addressing this problem (Wink, 2002). The Bavarian Minister-President and CSU leader Edmund Stoiber even demanded that the government should actively encourage higher levels of fertility among women (*Die Welt,* 9 August 2000). But these were long-term measures: indeed, it was the failure of the government to implement such measures in the previous thirty years, during which population decline was known to be taking place, which made the demographic situation at the turn of the millennium so stark (cf. *Die Zeit,* 9 January 2003). Clearly, if Germany was going to compensate for labour force shortfalls in the short to medium term, it would have to be at least in part through new labour migration.

In addition to the intellectual and economic arguments for new labour migration, the government was no doubt encouraged to press ahead with its plans by the continuing disarray of the opposition CDU. As a result of the party finance scandal, the CDU leader and its most capable politician, Wolfgang Schäuble, had been forced to resign after just eighteen months in office. His successor in April 2000 was Angela Merkel, the first woman and eastern German to lead a major political party. This background, combined with a circumspect attitude to religious values, meant that she did not fit easily into the (usually Catholic) conservative milieu from which much of the CDU's senior figures has been drawn; she had, for instance, voiced serious reservations over the use of the petition campaign. She therefore faced conservative rivals in the form of CDU/CSU parliamentary party leader Friedrich Merz, and CSU leader Stoiber. All three soon found themselves in a three-way race to be the joint CDU/CSU chancellor candidate at the 2002 federal election. With *Ausländerpolitik* a key area where her authority could be challenged, the sense of disunity within the CDU/CSU of the past fifteen years was all set to continue.

Nonetheless, following the election in North Rhine-Westphalia, the CDU/CSU leadership reacted quickly and with purpose to the changed nature of the debate, not least in order to realign itself with business interests as one of the party's most important political constituencies. Suddenly, high-skilled migration was no longer the issue: of course Germany needed to attract the brightest and the best, who by definition would only ever arrive in small numbers. Nor was the question of whether Germany was a country of immigration still central to policy, although it remained prominent within the CSU. The two parties now declared their support for an immigration law to regulate such migration (*Migration und Bevölkerung,* June 2000). Instead, the CDU/CSU now

concentrated its efforts on making its agreement to new labour migration dependent on further asylum reform and, most importantly in the
context of this analysis, linking such migration to better integration.

The salience of integration

In many ways, integration has represented the holy grail of *Ausländerpolitik* for over twenty years. Ever since being adopted as one of the
three principal policy goals in the in the 1977 commission, all governments and all parties have wrestled with its definition. In this, they were
certainly aided by the fact that the notion of integration remained
nebulous in the commission's report. As Katzenstein notes, 'West
German policymakers advocated a vaguely defined policy of social
integration that permitted a broad spectrum of interpretations by all
the relevant policy actors' (1987: 219).

In theory, integration consists of both immigrant and host society
modifying their behaviour around universally accepted norms and standards; it does not consist of a unilateral adaptation of the immigrant to
the host society, which is assimilation. But neither does it imply the
multicultural ideal of both parity and celebration of other cultures
(Parekh, 2000), an aspiration which was supported, at least in principle,
by the Greens throughout the 1980s (Murray, 1994; see also Cohn-Bendit
and Schmid, 1992).

The question of what integration, especially in terms of citizenship,
means in practice is of course a very complex one. Where precisely
should the line be drawn between what each side should expect and
tolerate of each other? Throughout the period under consideration in
this book, this question has been interpreted very differently by different
parties. For Peter O'Brien, the difference between Left and Right in the
response to this question comes down to whether the state or the immigrant was expected to 'make the first move'. For the SPD and the Greens,
it was traditionally the government which should take the lead in inclusion, by providing secure residence permits, voting rights (see Chapter
3) and easy access to citizenship. For the CDU and especially the CSU,
it was to be left to the individual foreigner alone to decide when to apply
for a secure residence permit or naturalisation. As O'Brien argues:

> Proposals from the Left imperiously assigned foreigners rights and status
> without ever giving them the opportunity to decide whether they wanted

them or not. A truly liberal democratic state had to protect the individual's free choice. This emphasis on migrants' right to choose became the hallmark of the CDU's policy and accordingly turned up in practically every party statement on immigration. (O'Brien, 1996: 97)

Crucially, this also meant that the foreigner would be required to demonstrate that he or she had achieved the level of integration required to be granted the status he or she aspired to. This requirement was particularly evident in naturalisation policy, not least in the 1977 Guidelines on Naturalisation (cf. Chapter 2). Thus the CDU/CSU emphasised again and again during the 1980s and 1990s that naturalisation could only take place once the integrative process had been completed, and could not constitute a step towards this ultimate goal. Similarly, the CDU/CSU consistently rejected *ius soli* on the basis that its automatism provided no guarantee of integration, and dual citizenship on the basis that successful integration in Germany precluded a formalised attachment to another country via nationality.

This insistence that only descent from German parents could automatically guarantee integration, and that anyone else, even if born in Germany, would need to prove their integration before obtaining citizenship, certainly had some anachronistic ethnocultural undertones about it. It also did little to promote the acceptance, and hence the integration, of non-nationals in German society. If naturalisation was available only at the end of integration, then it followed that any foreign resident in Germany was either not yet integrated, did not want to be integrated or, even worse, could not be integrated. For why would anyone who was integrated *not* want to become a German citizen?

Although the introduction of the new citizenship law in 2000 did change the emphasis of naturalisation policy, it did so only partially, by limiting *ius soli* and introducing new requirements for language skills and constitutional loyalty (see Chapter 4). In its aftermath, there was a discernible shift in emphasis onto integration in a broader sense, which drew on renewed evidence that non-national residents in Germany as a whole were on the way to becoming a socio-economically marginalised group in society, with higher unemployment, lower incomes, worse (and more expensive) housing and lower levels of formal education (Table 5.1).

As in the case of demographic changes, this too was not a new revelation. Ever since 1975, practitioners had been warning that government needed to do more to promote the socio-economic integration of non-nationals, especially with regard to their language skills and

Table 5.1 Selected socio-economic indicators for non-national and German populations

	Non-nationals		Germans	
Average living space per person (m²)	31 (1998)	29 (1985)	46 (1998)	39 (1985)
Average rent per m² (DM)	11.51 (1998)	–	10.69 (1998)	–
Household poverty rate[a] (%)	26 (1998)	33 (1996)	11 (1998)	14 (1995)
Infant mortality (per 000 live births)	5.4 (1999)	8.0 (1992)	4.4 (1999)	5.9 (1992)
School leavers with University entrance (*Abitur*) (%)	9.7 (1999)	8.9 (1994)	25.5 (1999)	25 (1994)
School leavers with no qualifications (%)	9.3 (1999)	20.4 (1994)	8.0 (1999)	7.8 (1994)
Unemployment rate (western Germany only) (%)	16.4 (2000)	20.4 (1997)	7.8 (2000)[b]	11.0 (1997)[b]
Social security recipients (*Sozialhilfeempfänger*) (%)	8.1 (1999)	–	2.9 (1999)	–

Notes:
[a] Defined as households with under 50 per cent average incomes (western Germany only).
[b] Unemployment rate for entire population (i.e. including non-nationals).
Source: Collated from data in Beauftragte der Bundesregierung (2002: 192, 315–18, 322–3, 408).

educational attainments (Meier-Braun, 2002: 44–5; 115–19). Katzenstein, too, had noted the divergence between education levels and unemployment rates for non-nationals compared with those for the entire population (1987: 229, 230–2). In December 2001, more evidence was provided in the form of the Programme for International Student Assessment (PISA), which had been run by the Organisation for Economic Cooperation and Development (OECD). This showed that the educational outcomes of children with a migration background were clearly lower than those of Germans, although a child's social background, regardless of nationality, was shown to be an even stronger determinant (Beauftragte der Bundesregierung, 2002: 182–3; *Migration und Bevölkerung*, January 2002). Other studies have revealed that the German-language competence of second- and third-generation nonnationals is actually decreasing (cf. *Welt am Sonntag*, 17 February 2002; Hansen, 2003: 92–3). Such findings have only helped to reinforce fears, especially among conservative opinion, that German society is threatened by the emergence of parallel societies in immigrant ghettos, in which Islamic fundamentalism can flourish. Although some commentators have argued that immigrant integration in reality has been better than its reputation (see for instance Thränhardt, 1995b; Meier-Braun, 2002: 22–9), this sense of fear was captured particularly well by the magazine *Der Spiegel*, which entitled a report on the failures of integration policy as 'The underbelly of the republic' (*Der Spiegel*, 4 March 2002).

Crucially, these deficits in integration have not been limited to non-nationals. Ethnic Germans too have developed into a clearly identifiable marginal group, despite their access to citizenship and over DM 1.1 bn being spent on their integration in 2001. While these sums have been cut dramatically since the early 1990s, they were still roughly ten times the total amount allocated for non-nationals (Beauftragte der Bundesregierung, 2002: 46). Here too, language skills have been shown to be in short supply: while ethnic Germans themselves have to prove their competence in German, their dependants, who in 2001 made up over 75 per cent of this form of immigration, do not. What is more, ethnic Germans have had great difficulties in integrating into the labour market, either because their skills are not required in Germany or because qualifications gained in the former Soviet Union are frequently not recognised (Münz and Ohliger, 1998). In consequence, both unemployment and crime is rife, prompting repeated calls from mainly SPD politicians that their immigration should be curbed further (*Der Spiegel*, 24 February 2003).

The Leitkultur controversy

Politically, this new concern with integration was skilfully exploited in autumn 2000 by Friedrich Merz, the leader of the CDU/CSU *Fraktion* in the *Bundestag*. In a newspaper interview in October 2000, he argued that non-ethnic German immigrants (*Zuwanderer*) should be expected to adopt Germany's 'dominant culture' (*Leitkultur*), which he later defined as adherence to the normative values contained in Germany's Basic Law (*Die Welt*, 25 October 2000). In doing so, Merz put the cat among the pigeons. As well as prompting an anguished intellectual debate over what it actually meant to be German (cf. Klusmeyer, 2001), his initiative also had the (perhaps not unintended) effect of causing maximum embarrassment to Angela Merkel and her allies, thereby raising the value of Merz's stock within the party. While she herself was cautious about the use of such a provocative term, conservative politicians in both the CDU and especially the CSU applauded Merz's frankness in emphasising that the duty for integration lay firmly with the immigrant (*Der Spiegel*, 6 November 2000).

Commissions galore: the development of immigration concepts, 2000–1

By summer 2000, it was evident that the government had decided to regulate immigration formally before the end of the legislative period in September 2002. This was clearly an ambitious project, which was set to supersede the *Ausländergesetz* as Germany's primary legislative instrument in immigration policy. It was also set to be the most comprehensive piece of legislation in this policy field ever to have been passed in Germany, in that it aimed to regulate both immigration and integration. By definition, this also included the connected issues of asylum and family reunification, with all the potential for party political conflict that these entailed.

The following twelve months saw a veritable flurry of activity, as all the parties, several societal groups and even some *Länder* scrambled to set up working groups to flesh out detailed proposals on the various elements of the law (Angenendt, 2002).[4] Of these, Interior Minister Schily's decision to convene his own independent commission on immigration in June 2000 attracted the most attention, both because it would report to Schily himself and because of its explicit cross-party membership. Its brief was to develop 'practical solutions and recommendations for a reform of all aspects of *Ausländerpolitik*' (Schily, quoted in *Migration und Bevölkerung*, July 2001). But Schily's real coup was to persuade the highly respected former CDU speaker of the *Bundestag*, Rita Süssmuth, who had long been a liberal voice inside the party, to chair the commission and thereby make its claim to non-partisanship credible. This was reflected in the remainder of the commission's membership, which included representatives from all main parties except the CSU and PDS, as well as from churches, unions, employers, local authorities and the UNHCR. The last member to be appointed was the Turkish-born travel entrepreneur Vural Öger, who was thus the first person of immigrant background to have a direct input into government thinking. Schily also insisted that no active frontline politician should be appointed as a party representative. He thereby neatly sidestepped the danger that the commission would be taken over by party political disputes, which would also have threatened to tie his hands when it actually came to formulating a bill. For its part, the CDU was furious and openly demanded that Süssmuth resign from the commission, which she duly declined to do. In response, the party in July 2000 set up its own, partisan commission on immigration, which was to be headed by the self-confessed moderate Minister-President of the Saarland, Peter Müller.

During the remainder of 2000 and the first half of 2001, the various party bodies and the two commissions carried out their work. However, the publication of the CDU and Süssmuth commissions' reports in June and July 2001, respectively, showed that initial hopes for a cross-party consensus were unlikely to be fulfilled. On the one hand, both commissions agreed that the key to better integration lay in better language skills. This meant that government policy had to depart from its traditionally voluntary model of language learning to a much more formal, structured approach of the kind which had been introduced, albeit with a varying degree of success, in the Netherlands in 1998 (Böcker and Thränhardt, 2003). Consequently, such integration courses were quickly incorporated into the various legislative proposals. On the other hand, their conclusions differed fundamentally in the areas of labour migration, family reunification and asylum. Overall, the Süssmuth commission argued that Germany would need immigration for demographic reasons, while the CDU commission maintained that new immigration should be prevented as far as possible (cf. Hailbronner, 2001). Table 5.2 summarises the two commissions' proposals on these issues, and compares them with the Interior Ministry's subsequent draft bill of August 2001.

Negotiating the *Zuwanderungsgesetz*

The publication of the two commissions' reports marked the end of the period of conceptual thinking by the two large parties, and signalled the start of the more messy political process of building the necessary majority to achieve a legislative outcome. This was by no means an easy task and was not comparable with past experiences in *Ausländerpolitik*. The reform of the *Ausländergesetz* in the late 1980s depended primarily on the coalition parties reaching an agreement, which did admittedly take a long time. But once this had been achieved, their twin majorities in both chambers of parliament meant the outcome of the law was

Table 5.2 Summary of main proposals for the *Zuwanderungsgesetz*, 2001

	Süssmuth commission (1)	CDU commission (2)	Interior Ministry draft (3)
High-skilled labour migration	Yes, selected by points-based system. Initial quota of 20,000 for permanent migration; additional migration to cover skills shortages	Yes, selected by points-based system, but only if deemed necessary	Yes, selected by points-based system, but only if deemed necessary
Low-skilled labour migration	No	No	No
Asylum policy	Recognition of non-state agents of persecution and gender-related grounds for asylum	No recognition of non-state agents of persecution and gender-related grounds for asylum; shorter appeals process	No recognition of non-state agents of persecution and gender-related grounds for asylum; scrapping of *Duldung*[a]
Maximum age for *Kindernachzug*	18	Preferably 6, but no more than 10	12, although 18 for children of high-skilled labour migrants
Integration courses	600 hours' compulsory classes	600 hours' compulsory classes	630 hours' compulsory classes
Residence framework	Simplification suggested, but no further details	Not mentioned	Reduction of residence titles from 5 to 2. EU nationals no longer need residence permits

Note: [a] The *Duldung* is a temporary but renewable stay of deportation, often on humanitarian or practical grounds. It is mostly valid only for short periods of time, and is commonly issued to failed asylum seekers. See also Chapter 4, n. 4 (p. 109)
Source: Collated from von Wilamowitz-Moellendorf and Wolffs (2001).

never really in doubt. In the formulation of the citizenship law in early 1999, there was little real disagreement between the coalition parties, although the government lacked a *Bundesrat* majority after the Hesse election. But it still had to bring on board only the smaller FDP, which was ideologically relatively sympathetic to the government's plans, in order to ensure success.

By contrast, in the case of the *Zuwanderungsgesetz*, the SPD had to build a majority to include both the coalition partner and the main opposition party. With the number of *Bundesrat* votes for the government smaller than it was in 1999 at the time of the citizenship decision, the backing of the CDU/CSU was quite simply a prerequisite for success. But this in turn threatened to alienate the Greens as the junior coalition partner, whose position on immigration was in some cases diametrically opposed to the CDU/CSU. For instance, while the CSU had argued in 2000 that the constitutional right to asylum should be replaced by an 'institutional guarantee', the Greens at their party conference that year actually adopted a return to the pre-1993 system of unrestricted access to asylum as party policy. Yet Schily, having invested considerable political capital into the issue, including convening the Süssmuth commission in the first place, could ill afford to simply revert to a 'non-decision' as the CDU/CSU had done when faced with similar opposition over citizenship between 1994 and 1998.

In a shrewd move, Schily began by making overtures to the CDU/CSU. In early August 2001, the Interior Ministry published its draft bill (*Referentenentwurf*) for the *Zuwanderungsgesetz*. There was widespread surprise when this was found to be based only partially on the Süssmuth commission's report, diverging considerably in asylum and family reunification policy. It thereby prompted speculation that the Ministry had in fact been working on the bill even before the Süssmuth commission had reported back (Angenendt, 2002: 42). More importantly, the draft (see Table 5.2, column (3)), particularly in these two areas, was unmistakably pitched at the CDU/CSU at the expense of the Greens. Schily clearly hoped to reach an agreement with the opposition, even if it meant provoking conflict within the coalition, which he no doubt calculated he could win.

The draft bill not only attracted the ire of the Greens, but was also rejected by the CDU and most strongly by the CSU, for whom it placed too much emphasis on new immigration (*Die Welt*, 5 September 2001). For their part, the Greens demanded improvements in asylum and family reunification policy and actually threatened to bring down the government over this issue. In a remarkable display of brinkmanship, Schily held out until 29 October 2001 before agreeing to include non-state and gender-based persecution as grounds for asylum (see Table 5.2) and to raise the maximum age for *Kindernachzug* to fourteen (and to eighteen for those with adequate language skills). Only then did the Greens' leadership promise their support (*Die Welt*, 30 October 2001).

But in the meantime, the terrorist attacks on New York and Washington had taken place on 11 September 2001. These events threatened to derail the *Zuwanderungsgesetz* project completely, as the resulting emphasis on internal security 'spilled over' into the agendas of new labour migration and integration. This was reinforced by the revelation that several of the terrorists had spent time in Germany prior to carrying out the attacks. In consequence, Schily fast-tracked two emergency packages of measures aimed at beefing up both internal and external aspects of Germany's security. Simultaneously, though, the momentum for *Zuwanderungsgesetz* was maintained, and the corresponding bill, which incorporated the Greens' amendments, was signed off by the federal cabinet on 7 November 2001.

With the legislative process now imminent, the political fault lines had once again emerged along familiar tracks. The SPD and Greens supported the *Zuwanderungsgesetz*, while the CDU/CSU rejected it, arguing that the law would mean more, not less, new immigration. The FDP and PDS, although initially opposed, later signalled their support in the *Bundesrat*. In substantive terms, four main points of contention between the main parties quickly became apparent. They were the extent of new labour migration, the format (and financing) of integration courses, the maximum age for *Kindernachzug* and the future of the asylum system, including the question of whether the grounds for recognition should be extended.

Throughout the parliamentary process, which began with the first reading of the bill on 13 December 2001 (Bundestagsdrucksache 14/7387; Deutscher Bundestag Plenarprotokoll 14/208), the government's search for a consensus with the CDU/CSU continued. But this was dealt a blow on 11 January 2002, when, after more than a year of wrangling, the CSU leader Edmund Stoiber won what was originally a three-horse race to become the joint CDU/CSU chancellor candidate for the 2002 election. This move effectively signalled the start of the election campaign and simultaneously reduced the chances for a compromise, as it was Stoiber's party, the CSU, which was most implacably opposed to the bill. The CDU/CSU no doubt also had one eye on opinion polls, which consistently provided evidence of widespread public disquiet over immigration. In June 2001, for instance, an Allensbach poll revealed that 53 per cent of respondents wanted any new law to reduce immigration; a further 28 per cent wanted the law to limit immigration to current levels (quoted in *Migration und Bevölkerung*, July 2001). Nonetheless, Stoiber's unswerving rejection of the law was by no means universally accepted within the CDU, and the entire negotiation process of the bill was accompanied by a range of dissenting voices advising the party to compromise.

Meanwhile, the government considered how to proceed. With the coalition trailing in the polls and some figures in the CDU/CSU threatening to make immigration an issue in the federal election campaign, it was clear from the government's point of view that the issue had to be settled quickly. There were also more mundane tactical matters to factor in: even with the support of the three states in which the SPD governed with either the FDP or the PDS, the government could muster only thirty-one of the thirty-five votes necessary to pass the bill in the *Bundesrat* (see Table 5.3, p. 127). This level, too, was under threat: a *Land* election in Saxony-Anhalt was scheduled for 21 April 2002, at which the incumbent SPD government was predicted to suffer a heavy defeat. In order to ensure that the bill reached the final *Bundesrat* vote before then, the government therefore employed the tried-and-tested tactic in the history of *Ausländerpolitik* of getting its bill through parliament at breakneck speed. As Meier-Braun notes, 'never before had such a far-reaching bill been pushed through so quickly, despite clear parallels to Schäuble's *Ausländergesetz* of 1990' (Meier-Braun, 2002: 122).

The bill's progress through the *Bundestag* was therefore marked by the now established mixture of extremely tight deadlines and mutual recriminations between the main parties over their respective unwillingness to consider each other's proposals (details in Meier-Braun, 2002: 122–40). But while the coalition's majority meant that the approval of the *Bundestag* was certain, the federal government was still no nearer to building a majority in the *Bundesrat*. At the same time, the coalition partners were determined to avoid the horse-trading of the conciliation committee (*Vermittlungsausschuss*) that would follow a rejection by the *Bundesrat*, fearing that this would inevitably lead to an unsatisfactory compromise solution. So the two parties began to concentrate on prising one state away from the CDU/CSU bloc of votes, with the aim of repeating the government's tactical masterstroke of summer 2000, when it managed to buy off several states to ensure that its major tax reform was accepted (cf. Chapter 1). Their target was the eastern *Land* of Brandenburg, which not only had the necessary four votes to pass the bill, but was also governed by an SPD–CDU grand coalition. What was more, the senior CDU minister in Brandenburg, former general Jörg Schönbohm, had indicated that he might be persuaded to vote in favour of the bill if certain conditions were met. Therefore, in late February 2002, the SPD and Greens made a series of further concessions to the CDU/CSU, including an offer to reduce the limit for *Kindernachzug* back down to age twelve.

The new chancellor candidate Edmund Stoiber remained unimpressed and refused to accept the amended compromise offer. With the election now just seven months away, the CDU/CSU's position hardened into rejection not simply on substance, but also on principle. At the same time, the party leadership put massive pressure on Schönbohm not to be swayed by the government's latest charm offensive, as defeat in this high-profile issue threatened to get Stoiber's campaign for the all-important federal election off to the worst possible start.

While the bill's passage through the *Bundestag* was predictable in both its style and outcome, no-one could have foreseen the furore that was unleashed following the final vote in the *Bundesrat* on 22 March 2002. As this has implications for our understanding of the policy process and of semisovereignty, it is worth recounting it in greater detail. In the deciding moment, when Brandenburg was asked by the speaker to cast its vote, a unique instance of political theatre unfurled (details in *Der Spiegel*, 30 March 2002). In the first instance, Brandenburg's Social Affairs Minister Alwin Ziel (SPD) voted 'yes', and its Interior Minister Schönbohm (CDU) voted 'no'. Under Article 51 of the Basic Law, *Länder* are not permitted to split votes in the *Bundesrat*, so the speaker, Berlin's Mayor Klaus Wowereit, asked Brandenburg's Minister-President Manfred Stolpe (SPD) for clarification. He replied in the affirmative, to which Schönbohm, when asked again, did not explicitly vote 'no', instead stating that his views were already known. Therefore, Wowereit declared that Brandenburg had voted in favour of the bill. With the FDP and PDS supporting the government through their coalitions with the SPD in Rhineland-Palatinate, as well as in Berlin and Mecklenburg-Western Pomerania, respectively, the bill was accepted (Table 5.3).

Immediately, the normally sedate atmosphere of the *Bundesrat* was shattered as the CDU Minister-Presidents Bernhard Vogel (Thuringia) and Roland Koch (Hesse) erupted in anger and staged a walk-out from the chamber in protest at this chain of events. But what initially appeared to be a constitutional crisis was quickly unmasked as a political farce, in which not only the precise exchange between Wowereit, Schönbohm and Stolpe had been choreographed, but also, albeit independently, Koch and Vogel's outrage and protest.

Notwithstanding the unprecedented scenes in the *Bundesrat*, questions remained over whether Wowereit's interpretation of Brandenburg's votes conformed with the Basic Law's stipulation that these must be cast unanimously. The CDU/CSU made clear its intention to seek clarification of this issue in the Constitutional Court if Federal

Table 5.3 Results of the *Bundesrat* vote on the *Zuwanderungsgesetz*, 22 March 2002

Land (Votes)	Coalition	Result	Land (Votes)	Coalition	Result
Baden-Wüttemberg (6)	CDU–FDP	Abstain	Mecklenburg-Western Pomerania (3)	SPD–PDS	Yes
Bavaria (6)	CSU	No	North Rhine-Westphalia (6)	SPD–Greens	Yes
Berlin (4)	SPD–PDS	Yes	Rhineland-Palatinate (4)	SPD–FDP	Yes
Brandenburg (4)	SPD–CDU	Yes	Saarland (3)	CDU	No
Bremen (3)	SPD–CDU	Abstain	Saxony (4)	CDU	No
Hamburg (3)	CDU–FDP–Schill	Abstain	Saxony-Anhalt (4)	SPD	Yes
Hesse (5)	CDU–FDP	Abstain	Schleswig-Holstein (4)	SPD–Greens	Yes
Lower Saxony (6)	SPD	Yes	Thuringia (4)	CDU	No

Total votes in favour: 35; total against: 17; total abstentions: 17

Source: *Migration und Bevölkerung* (May 2002).

President Johannes Rau (SPD) signed it into law. When he did so on 20 June 2002, several CDU-led states challenged the *Zuwanderungsgesetz*'s legitimacy in the Constitutional Court. On 18 December 2002, just two weeks before it was due to come into force, the Court struck down the law, finding that the initial divergence between Ziel and Schönbohm's decisions in effect invalidated Brandenburg's votes, thereby denying the bill the necessary majority to become law.

Semisovereignty and the *Zuwanderungsgesetz*

Despite failing to make it onto the statute books before the end of this book's period of consideration in 2002, the broader debate over the *Zuwanderungsgesetz* marks a subtle, but significant shift in the history of *Ausländerpolitik*. Politically, the emphasis is no longer simply on the blanket restriction of immigration, but on the management of immigration and integration to Germany's best interests. For a country whose government was, as late as mid-1998, arguing that Germany was not a country of immigration, this has represented a remarkable turnaround. Despite permitting only very limited new labour migration, the new law's radical simplification of residence permits from five to two, as well as the introduction of integration courses, would have gone a long way towards formalising the reality of Germany as a country of immigration (Green, 2003). Indeed, so comprehensive was the *Zuwanderungsgesetz* that, in overall terms, it could have been the exception to the rule of incremental policy change and constituted a path defining moment in *Ausländerpolitik*. As it was, the SPD–Green government could only promise to reintroduce the bill unchanged in 2003, with the intention of now seeking an outcome through the conciliation committee between *Bundestag* and *Bundesrat*. The rejection of the *Zuwanderungsgesetz* therefore confirms previous patterns of path dependency by demonstrating how difficult it is to depart from an established set of policy choices without building a 'grand coalition' of political interests.

Meanwhile, the impact of the 'Green Card' has been, inevitably, incremental. Between their introduction in August 2000 and March 2002, fewer than 11,500 'Green Cards' had been awarded (Beauftragte der Bundesregierung, 2002: 310), well below the initial quota of 20,000. Even those who have taken up this opportunity have not always found it easy: there have been numerous instances of overzealous bureaucrats terminating 'Green Card' holders' residence at the earliest opportunity (*Der Spiegel*, 2 September 2002).

In fact, this low level of take-up raises the question of whether Germany has fully grasped the nature of the global competition for skills in which it professes to want to succeed. All of the labour migration systems discussed, whether the 'Green Card' or the Süssmuth commission's points' system, were based on the premise that a plentiful supply of highly qualified immigrant labour was available and only needed to be managed in Germany's interest. What the reality of the 'Green Card' has so far illustrated is that this supply of labour may be much lower than first expected. In other words, this experiment indicates that the brightest and best may simply not want to go and work in Germany.

It is not difficult to see why this might be the case. Compared with competitor nations such as the UK and especially the USA and Canada, Germany is at a clear disadvantage: in 2002, the possibilities for labour migration remained highly limited, residence legislation (not least for dependants) was extremely complex, migrants had the linguistic disadvantage of having to learn German and the bureaucracy was both inflexible and unsympathetic. Perhaps most of all, public discussions about *Leitkultur* and recurrent media reports of attacks on asylum seekers and non-nationals especially in the eastern *Länder* did not help to paint a positive picture of Germany as land of opportunity for ambitious immigrants (cf. *Der Spiegel,* 8 May 2000).

As such, the 'Green Card' was probably never likely to be a runaway success. For Germany to successfully use the opportunity of new labour migration to meet its skills shortages and demographic challenges, it would have required a cultural and conceptual shift in perceptions to leave behind the decades-old political dogma of the ethnoculturally exclusive non-immigration country. Clearly, this could not have been achieved within just four years, although history may well pinpoint the 'Green Card' debate as the turning point in Germany's *Ausländerpolitik.*

Semisovereignty, too, has a central role to play in explaining the debates over immigration between 2000 and 2002. One of the most striking aspects of the events outlined above is the way in which the parties, rather than being mere nodes of the policy-making network, were almost constantly in electioneering mode during the Schröder government's first term in office. Thus, the prospect of winning the 1999 Hesse election was a key factor in determining the CDU's strategy against dual citizenship, while the 2000 North Rhine-Westphalian election provided a convenient focal point for its rejection of new labour migration. Moreover, the negotiations for and parliamentary passage of the *Zuwanderungsgesetz* coincided first with the extraordinary events of 11 September 2001, and then with the nomination of Edmund Stoiber as the CDU/CSU chancellor candidate and hence the start of the federal election campaign. Only between summer 2000 and 2001 did the *de facto* campaigning pause while the various parties and commissions deliberated their positions.

This near-constant focus on elections made it extremely unlikely that the parties would reach a compromise on an area as complex and as emotive as *Ausländerpolitik.* The process was further complicated by the range of opinions that were being expressed within the large parties, and especially the CDU, for which it proved difficult to arrive at a unified position. Indeed, three CDU parliamentarians voted with the SPD–Green government on the third and final reading of the *Zuwanderungsgesetz* on 1 March 2002 (Deutscher Bundestag Plenarprotokoll 14/222). Yet neither the CDU/CSU nor the SPD leadership could afford to be portrayed as giving way to the other in the run-up to an election when policy differences, no matter how symbolic they are, need to be accentuated, not softened. It was arguably this aim which prompted the two parties to (separately) stage the extraordinary scenes in the *Bundesrat* on 22 March 2002.

What was more, the substance of many of the issues was somewhat less than the level of party political conflict implied. At no point was it considered that Germany might actually have difficulties attracting the skilled labour it required, as the initial experience with the 'Green Card' indicates may be the case. Similarly, the entrenched nature of the dispute over *Kindernachzug* belied the fact that, had the CDU/CSU agreed to compromise on a maximum age of twelve, the difference in terms of extra new arrivals would have been no more than a few thousand (*Die Zeit*, 4 April 2002).

Once again, the absence of a significant parapublic institution in this field, within which many of these disputes could have been solved in a less politicised manner, was telling. However, there were two early indications of possible change for the future. First, the Süssmuth commission, with its explicit cross-party membership, was an direct attempt to inject a more rational tone from all corners of society into the debate, although its limited remit to provide recommendations meant that it did not possess the decision-making capacity which is normally a feature of parapublic institutions. Second, the *Zuwanderungsgesetz* envisaged the creation of a new Federal Office for Migration and Refugees (*Bundesamt für Migration und Flüchtlinge*), which would have had responsibility for identifying labour market shortages, the management of recruitment and the implementation of the new integration programmes. With such a comprehensive catalogue of competencies, this was clearly a parapublic institution in the making.

In institutional terms, two principal elements of Katzenstein's decentralised state played a key role in determining the fate of the *Zuwanderungsgesetz*. First, the *Bundesrat* was ultimately able to veto the law despite the government mustering the largest bloc of votes. Indeed, as Table 5.3 shows, once Brandenburg's votes are counted as abstentions, as the Constitutional Court ruled they should have been, there were actually fewer 'no' votes cast than either 'yes' votes or abstentions. With a veto threshold in this instance of just 25 per cent of votes cast, the rejection of the *Zuwanderungsgesetz* thus underlines the *Bundesrat's* potency as a limit on the federal government.

Second, the Constitutional Court was obviously instrumental in confirming the *Bundesrat's* status as a potential veto point in its judgement of 18 December 2002. But the implications of this ruling for semisovereignty go much further: it institutionalised the ability of the junior coalition partner to effectively 'spoil' a *Land*'s votes, merely by not casting these unanimously. Situations such as the *Bundesrat* vote on pensions reform in 2001, which was carried only when the SPD in Mecklenburg-Western Pomerania simply overruled its junior coalition partner's insistence on abstention to vote in favour, will therefore potentially be even rarer in the future. If anything, the *Zuwanderungsgesetz* controversy has enhanced the *Bundesrat*'s ability to act as a veto point for parties in opposition at federal level.

Lastly, the case of the *Zuwanderungsgesetz* makes for an interesting comparison with the Kohl government's non-decision over citizenship. As was argued above, a mini-path dependence was in operation: once Interior Minister Schily had convened his immigration commission, it became politically impractical for him to retreat into a non-decision. In turn, once the government was committed to the law, it did all it could, including once again pushing the bill through the *Bundestag* at a breath-taking pace and its attempt to finesse the CDU in the *Bundesrat*, to ensure that it was successful. Clearly, such a strategy entails the risk that the bill is not successful, as was the case here. But it also confirms that the federal government is first among equals in policy-making terms. Although it does not have the exclusive right of initiation of bills, it is *de facto* the moral leader: between 1949 and 1998, it sponsored over 75 per cent of all laws passed (quoted in Rudzio, 2000: 274). As a result, it can shape the policy agenda and debate decisively if it chooses to take the initiative. Thus, in the specific case of the *Zuwanderungsgesetz*, Chancellor Schröder's bold, if ultimately modest, proposal for new labour migration in 2000 completely changed the framework of debate. More-over, throughout the summer and autumn of 2001, it was the government which was setting the pace at all times, first with the bill itself and then with various amendments. In doing so, it was clearly to Schily's advantage that he was not limited to pre-arranged parameters by a coalition treaty. But the point was that the CDU/CSU opposition was simply left to react to them. One cannot help but wonder how different Germany's citizen-ship law might be had the CDU/CSU taken the initiative and chosen to set the terms of the debate between 1994 and 1998.

Notes

1 The term '*Zuwanderung*' had been introduced by CDU/CSU politicians

during the 1990s in place of the more conventional description for immigration of *Einwanderung*. Joppke (1999: 97–8) distinguishes between the terms as follows: '*Zuwanderung*, the term preferred by restrictionists, means unwanted immigration that is tolerated for constitutional and moral–political reasons. *Einwanderung*, by contrast, connotes actively solicited, wanted immigration.'

2 The 1990 *Ausländergesetz* had introduced a bewildering range of residence titles to cover different purposes of residence in Germany: *Aufenthaltsbewilligung* (a temporary permit for tourists and students); *Aufenthaltsbefugnis* (for humanitarian purposes); *befristete Aufenthaltserlaubnis* (limited residence permit for ordinary residence); *unbefristete Aufenthaltserlaubnis* (unlimited residence permit, available after five years' residence); *Aufenthaltsberechtigung* (residence entitlement, available after eight years' residence).

3 The scheme's name 'Green Card', which was borrowed from the USA, is in fact a misnomer: in the USA, the Green Card grants permanent residence status. The closest American equivalent to the German 'Green Card' is the H1-B visa.

4 The various concepts for the *Zuwanderungsgesetz* can also be accessed in full via: www.migration-info.de/informationen/index.htm.

6

Evaluating *Ausländerpolitik* and semisovereignty

The Constitutional Court's decision in December 2002 to overturn the *Zuwanderungsgesetz* marks the end of this book's empirical analysis. The preceding four chapters have traced the development of *Ausländerpolitik* in Germany over a period spanning more than four decades. Chapter 2 showed how the path dependency of Germany's self-perception as a non-immigration country was established, and how this was translated into policy principles in the 1965 *Ausländergesetz*, the 1977 and 1983 commissions on *Ausländerpolitik*, the 1977 Guidelines on Naturalisation and the 1981 Guidelines on Family Reunification. Chapter 3 then illustrated how difficult the Interior Minister Friedrich Zimmermann found it to depart from these positions during the mid-1980s in order to introduce a different, more restrictive policy paradigm. Similarly, Chapter 4 examined the persistence of norms in naturalisation policy, despite concerted efforts by (this time) the SPD–Green government to introduce a liberal citizenship regime in 1999. Finally, Chapter 5 discussed how new, exogenous pressures in the form of skills shortages and demographic developments posed a real challenge to the political orthodoxy, which will remain on the agenda despite the failure of the *Zuwanderungsgesetz* in 2002.

Inevitably, it has not been possible to cover all aspects of *Ausländerpolitik* fully. As Table 1.1 (p. 2) showed, this is a policy area of great complexity, whose framework is moreover widely fragmented in a maze of laws and regulations. In consequence, the emphasis here has been on family reunification, labour migration, residence policy and citizenship. This has meant that two other major themes in immigration policy – asylum and ethnic Germans – have been addressed only in broad terms; the formulation of various legal instruments which regulate these areas in detail, such as the numerous Asylum Procedural Laws passed since 1978, have not been subject to scrutiny here. Similarly, it has not been feasible within the confines of this analysis to conduct a full investigation into the ideological roots of the parties' various policy positions. This question is of course particularly important for understanding the parties' starting positions in the policy-making process. So far, apart from some stimulating individual studies (e.g. Murray, 1994; O'Brien, 1996; Sutherland, 2001; see also König, Blume and Luig, 2003), it is an area that has been less well researched.

Instead, the focus of this investigation has been to explore whether the policy-making process can account for outcomes in *Ausländerpolitik*, and if so, whether its explanatory reach is limited to 'fine details' (Brubaker, 1992: 185), or whether it can account for rather more. In other words, a central aim of this book is to establish what political science has to offer in terms of explaining outcomes in contemporary Germany's immigration, residence and citizenship policy.

Not surprisingly, this book's answer is 'quite a lot'. By drawing on Peter Katzenstein's model of semisovereignty, one of the most complete and coherent models of governance in Germany, this book has argued that study of the policy-making process provides profound insights into timing and content of policy which, far from being mere details, are fundamental for determining policy output. In particular, this study challenges Brubaker's historically based claim (1992: 185) that policy outcomes are stable because of a widespread elite consensus over conceptions of nationhood. While this may have been the case for the nineteenth and first half of the twentieth centuries, the picture becomes more complex from the 1970s onwards. Thus, as the previous chapters have shown, the reason for the broad consistency in policy, notwithstanding some significant incremental changes, lies not in consensus, but in the results of the policy-making process. On the contrary, the fundamental disagreements over citizenship policy, as well as over Germany's self-definition as a non-immigration country, have shown that there has been anything but an elite consensus, at least at the symbolic level of politics, over the past twenty-five years.

Semisovereignty and *Ausländerpolitik*

But how has the semisovereign model of governance contributed to our understanding of *Ausländerpolitik* as illustrated by the three case studies? Essentially, the model posited that decentralised state institutions and centralised societal interests would interact consensually within three

main network nodes, consisting of political parties, cooperative federalism and parapublic institutions, to produce gradual policy change, or
incremental outcomes. Indeed, in Katzenstein's original study, migrant
labour was one of the six case studies which best fitted the model.
Table 6.1 compares institutions and outcomes in the mid-1980s and at
the turn of the millennium.

Table 6.1 The institutional structures of *Ausländerpolitik*

Institutional structures	Mid-1980s	2000
Decentralised state	Yes	Yes
Centralised society	Yes	Formally yes, but with little influence
Parapublic institutions	Yes	No
Party conflict	No	Yes
Segmentation tendencies	Yes	Formally yes, but often not in practice
Incremental policy change	Yes	Yes

Note: Categories and 1980s classification taken from Katzenstein (1987: 363).

As Table 6.1 shows, much had changed in the institutional structures
of *Ausländerpolitik* by 2000. Since the mid-1980s centralised societal
actors have had no significant role to play in policy-making for the
various issues outlined above. As was noted in Chapter 1, this relatively
unusual situation in German politics can be explained in part by the
unique nature of *Ausländerpolitik*: the actual subjects of the policy,
Germany's non-national population, have no voice in the political
process and no dedicated interest groups, and are only partially represented by German interests such as churches and unions.

Neither have parapublic institutions enjoyed any real role in this area
over the same period, which can be put down to two factors. First, the
policy agenda changed from labour market management, in which a
powerful parapublic institution in the form of the Federal Labour Office
(*Bundesanstalt für Arbeit*) had been present, to immigration control and
legal integration, in which parapublic institutions, with the exception
of the Federal Office for the Recognition of Foreign Refugees, did not
feature prominently. Second, because the federal government maintained that Germany was not a country of immigration, this new agenda
was in effect an informal one; it thereby made the establishment of a
new, dedicated parapublic institution to manage it superfluous. As such,
the office of the *Ausländerbeauftragte* was a poor substitute, given its

small size, lack of resources, organisational marginalisation within the Labour Ministry and limitation to a consultative role.

Overall, the absence of a major parapublic institution, combined with the marginal relevance of societal actors, has had an appreciable impact on policy-making patterns in this sector, as other, more overtly political actors sought to take its place. Initially, the gap in the institutional configuration left by the shift in the policy agenda was quickly filled by the Interior Ministry, whose leadership sought to impose a quite restrictive agenda on *Ausländerpolitik* during the 1980s. This agenda's failure in 1988 was so ignominious that the coalition parliamentary parties began to take on a much more activist role in policy formulation, which continued right up until the 1998 federal election. But as a result, the sector's policy style changed irrevocably, as the increased politicisation and polarisation of *Ausländerpolitik*, which had already begun in the late 1970s, came to dominate. Henceforth, there was no real notion of a 'rationalist consensus' (Dyson, 1982) or a 'unity of intentions' (Bulmer, 1989) in policy-making, and little evidence of a normative pressure towards consensus based around centripetal outcomes. Indeed, Chapters 3 and 4 have described how on two occasions there was no incentive for key protagonists to reach an outcome at all. Instead, high levels of party conflict have come to characterise this policy area, especially in the parliamentary process. In each of the three case studies, the federal government, regardless of its political composition, ignored the established norms and practices in German politics to push its respective bills through parliament at astonishing speed and against all protests from opposition parties and societal interests. Of course, such protests must have sounded rather hollow to the SPD–Green government in 1999 and 2002 given the CDU/CSU–FDP's tactics during the formulation of the 1990 *Ausländergesetz*.

At least in part, this polarisation can be put down to changes in the party system during the 1980s. These saw Germany's traditional 'triangular' party system, which almost by definition promotes centripetal outcomes, replaced by a 'two-bloc' system in which parties were forced to compete not only between blocs, but also within their bloc. This structural change to party competition came on top of an increased frequency of elections since the halcyon days of consensus in *Ausländerpolitik* in the 1970s: first, direct elections to the European Parliament (EP), with all their protest vote potential for extremist parties, were introduced in 1979, and the addition of five new *Länder* after unification in 1990 further added to the frequency of sub-national elections. By the mid-1990s, this meant that the next electoral test for the federal government, whether it takes place at *Land*, federal or even European level, was rarely more than a few months away. By itself, this feature of German politics has created very little incentive for parties, who therefore constantly need to mobilise their core supporters, to depoliticise the issue. This practically constant sense of electioneering has also impacted on the persistence of Katzenstein's so-called 'segmentation tendencies', which were less obvious in the late 1980s and 1990s. Despite a widely fragmented legal framework, parties have been keen to pick up on highly specific issues such as asylum immigration, criminal foreigners, local voting rights or the *Leitkultur* debate. In turn, these have regularly come to 'spill over' into the entire policy area, usually to the detriment of the vast majority of non-nationals who are law-abiding and long-term residents.

In contrast to parapublic institutions and centralised society, the decentralisation of the state has clearly been in evidence since the mid-1970s. In combination with political parties, the institutions of the state have played a major role in determining both timing and scope of policy outcomes. Thus, coalition politics foiled the CSU's restrictionist plans during the 1980s (Chapter 3) and, during the 1990s, prevented a new citizenship law being passed in spite of the existence of a mathematical majority (Chapter 4). During the negotiations for the *Zuwanderungsgesetz*, coalition politics, the Interior Ministry's ministerial autonomy and the Constitutional Court all played a role in limiting policy change.

But it is particularly the role of federalism as the key counterbalance to the federal government's scope for action which is brought out by the case studies. In the formulation of the *Ausländergesetz* in 1989 and early 1990, the possibility of losing its *Bundesrat* majority undoubtedly played a role in concentrating the CDU/CSU–FDP coalition's minds on actually reaching an agreement. It also ensured that the bill's legislative passage was completed literally days before the government's *Bundesrat* majority was in fact lost at the 1990 Lower Saxony election. During the mid-1990s, the prospect of having to negotiate a citizenship policy not only with the FDP but also with the SPD's majority in the *Bundesrat* offers a convincing explanation of why the CDU/CSU, as the actor whose position represented the least departure from the status quo, preferred a non-decision as the best outcome politically. In 1999, the effect of federalism was even more pronounced, when the SPD–Green government's defeat in Hesse spelled the end of the federal government's plans for general dual citizenship. Lastly, the case of the *Zuwanderungs-*

gesetz illustrates perfectly the *Bundesrat*'s ability to act as a veto point in German politics.

Yet by 2000, despite the considerable evolution of the institutional structure since the mid-1980s, and despite a much higher level of politicisation, outcomes remained broadly incremental. More than any other, it is this feature which confirms the continued ability of the semisovereign model to explain the nature of *Ausländerpolitik*. In all the case studies which have been analysed in this book, policy changes have not once constituted major departures from the patterns which were established prior to 1982. The 1990 *Ausländergesetz* failed to go beyond the formalisation of existing administrative practice in residence policy and drew mainly on the 1983 commission's recommendations in naturalisation policy. The impact of the new citizenship law on naturalisations, notwithstanding the huge symbolic significance of the introduction of *ius soli*, has been much less than initially hoped. For all its importance in changing the nature of the debate, the 'Green Card' itself has done little to address either skills or demographic shortages in Germany. Even the changes to asylum and ethnic German immigration, which arguably constitute the most dramatic policy changes reviewed here, have still turned out to be relatively gradualist in practice and have hence failed to provide political closure in these areas.

This constancy in policy outcomes has certainly not been the result for the parties' want of trying. At various stages during the 1980s and 1990s, both conservatives and liberals attempted to redefine elements of *Ausländerpolitik* according to their own conceptions. But whether it was the restriction of residence rights or the introduction of dual citizenship, any major departure from established norms was possible only in a 'grand coalition' setting (Schmidt, 1996), of the kind represented by the 1992 asylum compromise. In the absence of a cross-party consensus, these kinds of changes could in practice always be blocked. Overall, this pattern of policy-making has meant that Katzenstein's assertion (1987: 228) that 'incremental policy-making ... dulled the edge of a conservative reorientation' in the early 1980s can be applied to the SPD–Green government too, at least in *Ausländerpolitik*.

It will be interesting to see how future institutional developments in this area impact on policy outputs. The return of labour migration to the agenda potentially spells a much greater role for unions and employers as representatives of economic interests. Similarly, Interior Minister Schily's plans for a major new parapublic institution in this area, the Federal Office for Migration and Refugees, could have a significant depoliticising effect on immigration and integration, for which it will be at least co-responsible. Most of all, *Ausländerpolitik* is likely to become defined to an ever-increasing degree by Germany's membership of the EU, as regulation of immigration by third-country nationals at EU level gains greater momentum. In this process, Germany's status as home to almost half of all third-country nationals in the EU will accord it particular significance.

Ausländerpolitik and semisovereignty

At the same time, the study of *Ausländerpolitik* itself provides new insights into the functioning of the semisovereign model of governance. Already, the role of path dependency for setting the framework against which incremental policy changes can be measured has been noted by other authors (see Chapter 1). The importance of this historical perspective is clearly illustrated by the story of *Ausländerpolitik* in the second half of the twentieth century.

Four additional aspects need to be highlighted. First, Katzenstein is right to focus on political parties as central actors in the mediation of individual actors' interests. But in reality, not all parties are equal. In *Ausländerpolitik*, it has been the parties in federal government, and not necessarily the largest parties, who have consistently been the most important, especially given the absence of a wide-ranging cross-party consensus in this area. In particular, the parliamentary parties (*Fraktionen*) in the *Bundestag* must be singled out. Thanks to their formal organisation and substantial funding, they are often formidable power bases, and hence actors in their own right. Under the Kohl government, the government's *Fraktionen* were not only important sources of policy initiatives, but also acted as the principal counterbalance to Interior Minister Zimmermann's restrictive agenda.

Second, the non-reform of citizenship between 1994 and 1998, as well as the negotiation of the *Zuwanderungsgesetz* between 2000 and 2002, emphasised the agenda-setting role of federal governments. In citizenship policy, Interior Minister Kanther was clearly content to put a non-decision at the centre of his agenda. By contrast, Interior Minister Schily showed how effective an activist approach can be. He was consistently able to push the Greens to the limits of their endurance over asylum, citizenship, family reunification and labour migration. At the same time, he was able to prevent the CDU/CSU from taking the political initiative over immigration throughout the negotiation of the *Zuwanderungsgesetz*. Admittedly, the SPD in government found it easier to set the agenda because, in contrast to the CDU/CSU, it was the median legislator for this policy area. But the implication for semisovereignty is that the federal government, or on occasions even an individual minister, by virtue of this choice of whether or not to take the initiative, is not just an actor among many, but the first among equals.

Third, the case studies have underlined the importance of the coalition status itself. Chapter 4 showed just how essential the coalition agreement was between 1994 and 1998 in limiting the parameters for policy outcomes. Moreover, the spectre of bringing down the government was an important factor in preventing the FDP from brokering its own deal over citizenship with the SPD and Green opposition between 1994 and 1998. Membership or otherwise of a coalition can therefore be important for limiting parties' policy preferences, as both enforced and voluntary withdrawal from such an agreement between elections brings with it real political and electoral costs. A good example of this was Jörg Schönbohm's determination not to jeopardise his party's coalition with the SPD in Brandenburg by openly disagreeing with his Minister-President (as opposed to the Social Affairs Minister) during the vote on the *Zuwanderungsgesetz* in the *Bundesrat* in 2002 (see *Der Spiegel*, 30 March 2002).

The fourth area where semisovereignty can be refined is in the role of the *Bundesrat* in national politics. Katzenstein's original argument emphasised the function of federalism in achieving consensus and not as a veto point for the opposition to block policy initiatives it does not like. But he too recognised that this might be an issue for the future (Katzenstein, 1987: 378), citing Lehmbruch's critique of the CDU/CSU opposition's tactics in the 1970s of using its *Bundesrat* majority to force concessions from the government (Lehmbruch, 1976). While there is certainly plenty of evidence to suggest that territorial interests regularly supersede the political interests of the parties at federal level (e.g. Jeffery, 1999; Renzsch, 1999), the three case studies of the *Ausländergesetz* in 1990, the citizenship law in 1999 and the *Zuwanderungsgesetz* in 2002 together tell a different story. Indeed, in each of these three cases, the *Länder* votes in the *Bundesrat* were cast unequivocally according to national party positions. This is illustrated very clearly in the case of the 2002 vote on the *Zuwanderungsgesetz* (Table 5.3): once Brandenburg's split vote had been interpreted correctly as a spoilt vote (i.e. an abstention), the individual voting patterns of all the *Länder* entirely reflected party political divisions at federal level. This may well be due to the high degree of political salience at federal level of *Ausländerpolitik* (cf. Bräuninger and König, 1999), which can supersede party political interests within the *Länder*. In addition, direct *Länder* interests in the first two case studies were in the main limited to administrative implementation.[1] But nonetheless, it means that in this policy area at least, the *Bundesrat* has become a useful vehicle for the federal opposition parties to mobilise against government policy.

The effectiveness of semisovereignty for *Ausländerpolitik*

In his comparative analysis of three states' ability to control immigration, Christian Joppke concludes that 'Germany is still an extreme case of self-limited sovereignty' (1999: 267). While his analysis refers principally to Germany's external sovereignty, it could just as easily be applied to Katzenstein's findings that the federal government's ability to act in an outright majoritarian manner is highly circumscribed by coalition politics, federalism, the Constitutional Court, centralised societal actors and parapublic institutions. But semisovereignty did more than just explain how and why policy outcomes were incremental in Germany. For Katzenstein, this model of governance epitomised the strength of the (undoubtedly very successful) West German model and constituted a key source of the country's democratic stability. In the context of post-unification Germany, it seems opportune to conclude this study with the question of whether semisovereign governance remains a source of strength in *Ausländerpolitik* today. In other words, can semisovereignty still provide workable policies to structure the opportunities and to meet the challenges posed by immigration?

In this respect, it is difficult to reach a positive conclusion. The entire notion that Germany was not a country of immigration both stifled debate and precluded a much earlier adjustment of residence and citizenship policy to the social reality of a highly settled and stable immigrant population. Even though the SPD–Green coalition consciously took leave of this notion when it entered government, the long-term effects of exclusion linger on. Not only has public opinion remained broadly sceptical of immigration but, as Chapter 5 has argued, the socio-economic profile of non-nationals has clearly remained below that of German citizens. Immigrants and their descendants also remain heavily underrepresented in public service, not least due to the nationality requirement for civil servant status (*Beamtentum*), and in politics too: it is likely to be years, if not decades, before a parliamentarian of immigrant origin can rise to reach ministerial rank in Germany. This sense of exclusion is epitomised by the experiences of Cem Özdemir, a German citizen since 1983 and member of the *Bundestag* for the Greens from 1994 to 2002, who tells of returning to Germany from abroad on several occasions and of being asked by border guards, after inspection of his parliamentarian's German diplomatic passport, how long he intended to stay in the country (Özdemir, 1999: 12–13).

The political insistence on Germany's self-image as a non-immigration country also hid a number of remarkable double standards. For instance, while recognised ethnic Germans from the former Soviet Union are now naturalised even before their arrival in Germany, long-term resident non-nationals have to undergo a long-winded and expensive procedure. Similarly, ethnic Germans are not required to give up their previous citizenship while dual citizenship as a rule is not permitted for other nationalities. Most astonishingly, especially given the debate about local voting rights in the 1980s, Germany's Election Law (*Bundeswahlgesetz*) allows its citizens who reside in other member states of the Council of Europe to continue voting in German elections indefinitely, and for up to ten years if living outside this area. As a result, millions of tax-paying residents of Germany are left disenfranchised, while expatriates throughout the world can continue to add their voice to the composition of the German government.

Notwithstanding the implications of such iniquities for notions of justice, semisovereignty has certainly struggled to produce policy outcomes to keep pace with the evolution of Germany's non-national population into a permanent minority. In particular, it is the tendency for punctuated incremental policy changes, each occurring only after a prolonged period of inactivity, which has caused the gap between policy necessity and policy reality to widen. Citizenship policy is a fine example of this: despite already acknowledging in 1984 that higher levels of naturalisation were necessary, it was to be another seven years before any policy liberalisation was introduced. The *Ausländergesetz*'s simplified naturalisation procedure was followed by further minor changes in 1993 as part of the asylum compromise, and then later by the mixed bag of changes which constituted the 1999 citizenship reform (Green, 2000). While these step-by-step liberalisations have certainly helped to increase naturalisations compared to the 1980s, Chapter 4 has shown how even these higher figures, once live births and net immigration have been factored in, have failed to make any impression on the number of non-nationals living in Germany. In terms of achieving the 1984 goal of higher naturalisations, Germany's citizenship policy is obviously having to run just in order to stand still.

In other areas of *Ausländerpolitik* too, semisovereignty has simply not been able to provide workable policy answers. For most of the period under consideration here, the largest party in German politics, the CDU/CSU, has been able to insist on its view that Germany does not need new immigration. But in reality, Germany cannot do without it, and must if anything reconcile itself to more rather than less of it. Skills shortages are unlikely to abate in the coming years, and without major new immigration in the next twenty years, Germany's demographic situation will spell ruin for not only its pension funds and health system, but its entire public finances. As Peter Müller, who headed the CDU's immigration commission in 2001, has noted in allusion to the traditional populist rallying cry '*Das Boot ist voll*', 'the problem is not that the boat is too full, but that it is getting ever more empty' (quoted in *Der Spiegel*, 30 March 2002). Unfortunately for the effectiveness of *Ausländerpolitik*, this insight did not ultimately translate into the necessary policy framework.

Nonetheless, perhaps a more profound change is nearer than might be expected. So far, parties have had little incentive to take heed of Germany's non-national community, as low levels of naturalisation for a long time meant that few of these could actually vote. However, with historically high numbers of foreigners becoming new citizens between 1998 and 2002, this trend is being reversed. By 2002, a total of around 500,000 Turks had been granted German citizenship and were consequently eligible to vote in that year's federal election. With a study by Wüst (2002) showing that around 80 per cent of naturalised *Ausländer* cast their vote for either the SPD or the Greens, this is fast becoming an important electoral constituency for the two parties. As the next federal election, scheduled for late 2006, is likely to be another close-run affair between the two party blocs, the political voice of former non-nationals in Germany is sure to grow ever louder.

Notes

1 However, it must be noted that, in financial terms, *Länder* interests are affected much more directly in other aspects of *Ausländerpolitik*, notably asylum policy.

Appendix: key data on non-nationals in Germany, 1991–2002

	1991	1992	1993
Foreign population (m) [a]	5.9	6.5	6.9
of which Turks (m)	1.8	1.9	1.9
of which EU citizens (m)	1.5	1.5	1.5
Foreigners' share of total population (%)	7.3	8.0	8.5
Foreigners' share of live births (%)	12.4	12.4	12.9
Foreigners with over eight years' residence (%)	60.5	55.3	52.5
with permanent residence status (%) [b]	39.9	37.2	36.1
Net migration (000)	+423	+593	+277
New asylum seekers (000)	256	438	323
Recognition rate (%) [c]	6.9	4.2	3.2
Non-EU dependant visas issued (000)	n/a	n/a	n/a
Ethnic German immigrants (000)	222	231	219
Unemployment rate, West only (%)	10.7	12.2	15.1
compared to overall rate (=100)	170	185	184
Total racially motivated crimes	2,400	6,300	6,700
Total naturalisations (000s) [d]	27	37	45
of which with dual citizenship (%)	24.5	20.4	37.6
Naturalisation rate (%) [e]	0.5	0.6	0.6
for Turks (%)	0.2	0.4	0.7

Notes:
[a] On 31 December of year given.
[b] Percentage holding unlimited residence permits (*unbefristete Aufenthaltserlaubnis*), residence entitlements (*Aufenthaltsberechtigung*) and EU residence permits.
[c] Percentage of initial decisions taken (Note: not applications made) which granted recognition on formal or humanitarian grounds (i.e. excluding temporary prevention of deportation on humanitarian grounds under Section 53 *Ausländergesetz*).
[d] Excluding naturalisations of ethnic Germans.

1994	1995	1996	1997	1998	1999	2000	2001	2002
7.0	7.2	7.3	7.4	7.3	7.3	7.3	7.3	7.3
2.0	2.0	2.0	2.1	2.1	2.1	2.0	1.9	1.9
1.8	1.8	1.8	1.8	1.8	1.9	1.9	1.9	1.9
8.6	8.8	8.9	9.0	8.9	8.9	8.9	8.9	8.9
13.1	13.0	13.3	13.2	12.7	12.4	6.5	6.0	n/a
n/a	53.4	54.2	55.3	59.0	61.0	64.4	65.7	67.2
41.2	43.0	44.4	46.2	48.3	49.2	44.7	51.3	51.3
+152	+225	+149	−22	−33	+118	+86	+273	+235
127	128	116	104	98	95	79	88	71
7.3	11.7	12.3	10.6	7.7	7.5	10.9	21.2	5.0
n/a	n/a	55	62	63	71	76	83	85
223	218	178	134	103	105	96	98	91
16.2	16.6	18.9	20.4	19.6	18.4	16.4	16.5	17.8
176	178	187	185	209	209	210	n/a	n/a
3,500	2,500	2,200	3,000	2,600	2,300	3,600	n/a	n/a
62	72	86	82	107	143	187	178	155
37.0	34.3	23.2	21.9	18.9	13.8	44.6	48.3	41.5
0.9	1.0	1.2	1.1	1.5	2.0	2.6	2.4	2.1
1.0	1.6	2.2	2.0	2.8	5.0	4.1	3.9	3.4

[e] Percentage of non-national population which is naturalised that year.
Sources: Collated and calculated from Beauftragte der Bundesregierung (2002); www.destatis.de; http://www.bafl.de; Bundesverwaltungsamt. Where no data is given, it is either not available or unknown.

Bibliography

Abromeit, H. (1992), *Der verkappte Einheitsstaat* (Opladen: Leske & Budrich)

Altmaier, P., E. von Klaeden and N. Röttgen (1995), *Grundsätze zur Reform des Staatsangehörigkeitsrechts. Positionspapier vom 06.10.95*, Bonn

Altmaier, P., E. von Klaeden and N. Röttgen (1996), *Initiative in der CDU für ein zeitgemäßes Staatsangehörigkeitsrecht*, Bonn

Andersen, U. and W. Woyke (1997) (eds), *Handwörterbuch des politischen Systems der Bundesrepublik Deutschland* (Bonn: Bundeszentrale für politische Bildung)

Angenendt, S. (1997) (ed.), *Migration und Flucht. Aufgaben und Strategien für Deutschland, Europa und die internationale Gemeinschaft* (Bonn: Bundeszentrale für politische Bildung)

Angenendt, S. (2002), 'Einwanderungspolitik und Einwanderungsgesetzgebung in Deutschland, 2000–2001', in K. Bade and R. Münz (eds), *Migrationsreport 2002* (Frankfurt a.M.: Campus)

AWO (Arbeiterwohlfahrt) (1989), *Vorläufige Stellungnahme zum Referentenentwurf zur Neuregelung des Ausländerrechts*, Bonn, 11 October

Bachrach, P. and M. Baratz (1970), *Power and Poverty, Theory and Practice* (New York: Oxford University Press)

Bade, K. (1994), *Ausländer, Aussiedler, Asyl* (Munich: Verlag C. H. Beck)

Barwig, K. (1988), 'Zur Diskussion um die Novellierung des Ausländerrechts', *Zeitschrift für Ausländerrecht*, 4/1988: 173–83

Barwig, K. (1989), 'Neuere Vorschläge zur Novellierung des Ausländerrechts', *Zeitschrift für Ausländerrecht*, 3/1989: 125–31

Baum, G. (1981), 'Aktuelle Probleme der Ausländerpolitik', *Zeitschrift für Ausländerrecht*, 1/1981: 7–12

Beauftragte der Bundesregierung für Ausländerfragen (2001), *Migrationsbericht der Ausländerbeauftragten* (Berlin and Bonn), available via: www.integrationsbeauftragte.de (accessed 28 May 2003)

Beauftragte der Bundesregierung für Ausländerfragen (2002), *Bericht der Beauftragten der Bundesregierung für Ausländerfragen über die Lage der Ausländer in der Bundesrepublik Deutschland* (Berlin and Bonn), available via: www.integrationsbeauftragte.de (accessed 28 May 2003)

Beauftragte der Bundesregierung für die Integration der ausländischen Arbeitnehmer und ihrer Familienangehörigen (1988), *Ausländerbeauftragte legt Vorschläge zur Novellierung des Ausländerrechts vor*, Mitteilungen No. 2/1988, 12 January

Beauftragte der Bundesregierung für die Integration der ausländischen Arbeitnehmer und ihrer Familienangehörigen (1989a), *Liselotte Funcke begrüßt Einigung auf Eckwerte zur Neuregelung des Ausländergesetzes*, Mitteilungen No. 6/1989, 21 April

Beauftragte der Bundesregierung für die Integration der ausländischen Arbeitnehmer und ihrer Familienangehörigen (1989b), *Neues Ausländerrecht bedarf einer breiten Diskussion*, Mitteilungen No. 17/1989, 25 October

Bischoff, D. and W. Teubner (1992), *Zwischen Einbürgerung und Rückkehr: Ausländerpolitik und Ausländerrecht in der Bundesrepublik Deutschland* (Berlin: Hitit Verlag)

BMA (Bundesminister für Arbeit und Sozialordnung) (1982), *Ausländerpolitische Beschlüsse der Bundesregierung*, Bonn

BMA (Bundesminister für Arbeit und Sozialordnung) (1986), *Integration der jungen Ausländer. Fortschreibung der Vorschläge des Koordinierungskreis 'Ausländische Arbeitnehmer' beim Bundesministerium für Arbeit und Sozialordnung vom 22. November 1979*, Bonn

BMI (Bundesministerium des Innern) (1988), *Entwurf für ein Gesetz zur Neuregelung des Ausländerrechts*, unpublished and unofficial manuscript, 1 February

Böcker, A. and D. Thränhardt (2003), 'Erfolge und Misserfolge der Integration – Deutschland und die Niederlande im Vergleich', *Aus Politik und Zeitgeschichte*, B26/2003: 3–11

Bommes, M. (1991), *Intressenvertretung durch Einfluß. Ausländervertretungen in Niedersachsen* (Osnabrück: Arbeitsgemeinschaft Kommunale Ausländervertretungen Niedersachsen)

Bräuninger, T. and T. König (1999), 'The checks and balances of party federalism: German federal government in a divided legislature', *European Journal of Political Research*, 36: 207–34

Breuilly, J. (1992), 'The national idea in modern German history', in J. Breuilly (ed.), *The State of Germany* (London: Longman)

Brubaker, R. (1992), *Citizenship and Nationhood in France and Germany* (Cambridge, MA: Harvard University Press)

Bulmer, S. (1989), 'Unity, diversity and stability: the "efficient secrets" behind West German public policy?', in S. Bulmer (ed.), *The Changing Agenda of West German Public Policy* (Aldershot: ASGP/Dartmouth)

Bundesratsdrucksache 402/93

Bundestagsdrucksachen 9/1574, 10/2071, 11/6321, 11/6541, 11/6955, 11/6960, 12/4533

Bundestagsdrucksachen 13/423, 13/465, 13/4948, 13/7417, 13/7511, 14/509, 14/535, 14/867, 14/7387, available via: www.bundestag.de (accessed 3 November 2002)

CDA (Christlich-Demokratische Arbeitnehmerschaft) (1988), *Partnerschaft und Integration: Thesen zur Novellierung des Ausländerrechts*, Bonn, 14 February 1988

Çelik, H. (1995), *Die Migrationspolitik bundesdeutscher Parteien und Gewerkschaften. Eine kritische Bestandsaufnahme ihrer Zeitschriften 1980–1990* (Bonn: Protext)

Chapin, W. (1997), *Germany for the Germans? The Political Effects of International Migration* (Westport, CT: Greenwood Press)

Cohn-Bendit, D. and T. Schmid (1992), *Heimat Babylon. Das Wagnis der multikulturellen Demokratie* (Hamburg: Hoffmann & Campe)

Cooper, A. (2002), 'Party-sponsored protest and the movement society: the CDU/CSU mobilises against citizenship law reform', *German Politics*, 11/2: 88–104

de Haan, E. (1988), *'Bewahrung des eigenen nationalen Charakters'. Darstellung der Gesetzesentwürfe des Bundesinnenministers für ein neues Ausländergesetz*, Rheinbach/Bonn, unpublished manuscript

de Haan, E. (1990), 'Ausländergesetz und Integration', in Beauftragte der Bundesregierung für die Integration der ausländischen Arbeitnehmer und ihre Familienangehörigen (ed.), *Bericht 99. Zur Situation der ausländischen Arbeitnehmer und ihrer Familien – Bestandsaufnahme und Perspektiven für die 90er Jahre*, 2nd edn, Bonn

Decker, F. (1982), *Ausländer im politischen Abseits* (Frankfurt a.M.: Campus)

Deutscher Bundesrat Plenarprotokoll 290/1/90

Deutscher Bundestag Innenausschuss (1990), *Stenographisches Protokoll über die 77. Sitzung des Innenausschusses*, Bonn, 14 February

Deutscher Bundestag Innenausschuss (1999), *Reform des Staatsangehörigkeitsrechts: Die parlamentarische Beratung* (Berlin: Deutscher Bundestag)

Deutscher Bundestag Plenarprotokolle 11/88, 11/195, 11/207

Deutscher Bundestag Plenarprotokolle 14/28, 14/37, 14/40, 14/208 and 14/222, available from 1996 onwards via: www.bundestag.de (accessed 3 November 2002)

DGB (Deutscher Gewerkschaftsbund) (1989), *Stellungnahme des Deutschen Gewerkschaftsbundes zum Referentenentwurf zur Neuregelung des Ausländerrechts des Bundesministeriums des Innern*, Düsseldorf, 13 October

Diakonisches Werk der Evangelischen Kirche in Deutschland (1989), *Ein Diskussionsbeitrag des Diakonischen Werkes der EKD zur Novellierung des Ausländergesetzes*, Stuttgart, 23 January

Dornis, C. (2002), 'Zwei Jahre nach der Reform des Staatsangehörigkeitsrechts', in K. Bade and R. Münz (eds), *Migrationsreport 2002* (Frankfurt a.M.: Campus)

Dyson, K. (1982), 'West Germany: the search for a rationalist consensus', in J. Richardson (ed.), *Policy Styles in Western Europe* (London: Allen & Unwin)

Edye, D. (1987), *Immigrant Labour and Government Policy: The Cases of the Federal Republic of Germany and France* (Aldershot: Gower)

Fahrmeier, A. (1997), 'Nineteenth-century German citizenships: a reconsideration', *The Historical Journal*, 40/3: 721–52

Faist, T. (1994), 'How to define a foreigner? The symbolic politics of immigration in German partisan discourse, 1978–1992', in M. Baldwin-Edwards and M. Schain (eds), *The Politics of Immigration in Western Europe* (Ilford: Frank Cass)

FORSA Poll 948/2356

Forschungsgruppe Wahlen (2000), *Politbarometer 1977–1999 auf CD-ROM* (Mannheim: Forschungsgruppe Wahlen)

Frankfurter Allgemeine Zeitung, 3 October 1987, 'Zimmermann will Ausländerrecht in diesem Jahr ändern'

Frankfurter Allgemeine Zeitung, 16 September 1995, 'FDP rückt von Forderung der "Kinderstaatszugehörigkeit" ab'

Frankfurter Allgemeine Zeitung, 17 April 1996, 'CSU lehnt Vorschläge zum Staatsbürgerschaftsrecht ab'

Frankfurter Rundschau, 21 January 1999, 'Optionsmodell entzweit Unionsfraktion'

Frankfurter Rundschau, 3 February 1999, 'Den Abweichlern von Landau droht der Einmarsch'

Frankfurter Rundschau, 10 February 1999, 'Deutschsein als Schicksal'

Frankfurter Rundschau, 21 May 1999, 'Lautstark gegen den Doppelpass'

Franz, F. (1990), 'Der Gesetzentwurf des Bundesregierung zur Neuregelung des Ausländerrechts', *Zeitschrift für Ausländerrecht*, 1/1990: 3–10

Franz, F. (1992), 'Zwischenbilanz des deutschen Ausländerrechts', *Zeitschrift für Ausländerrecht*, 4/1992: 154–61

Frey, M. (1982), 'Ausländerpolitik in der Bundesrepublik Deutschland', in M. Frey and U. Müller (eds), *Ausländer bei uns – Fremde oder Mitbürger?* (Bonn: Bundeszentrale für politische Bildung)

Geddes, A. (2000), *Immigration and European Integration* (Manchester: Manchester University Press).

Geiß, B. (2001), 'Die Ausländerbeauftragten der Bundesregierung in der ausländerpolitischen Diskussion', in E. Currle and T. Wunderlich (eds), *Deutschland – ein Einwanderungsland? Rückblick, Bilanz und neue Fragen* (Stuttgart: Lucius & Lucius).

Geißler, H. (1982) (ed.), *Ausländer in Deutschland – für eine gemeinsame Zukunft* (Munich: Olzog Verlag)

Geißler, H. (1991), 'Die bunte Republik – multikulturelles Zusammenleben im neuen Deutschland und das christliche Menschenbild', *Zeitschrift für Ausländerrecht*, 3/1991: 107–13

Geißler, H. (1993), 'Deutschland – ein Einwanderungsland?', in S. Iranbomy (ed.), *Einwanderbares Deutschland oder Vertreibung aus dem Wohlstandspa-radies?* (Frankfurt a.M.: Horizonte Verlag)

Gerhardt, W. (1997), 'Einwanderung kontrollieren – Eingliederung und Ein-bürgerung erleichtern', *Zeitschrift für Ausländerrecht*, 3/1997: 107–10

Göbel-Zimmermann, R. (2003), 'Das neue Staatsangehörigkeitsrecht – Erfahrun-gen und Reformvorschläge', *Zeitschrift für Ausländerrecht*, 2/2003: 65–75

Green, S. (1999), 'The 1998 German Bundestag election: the end of an era', *Parliamentary Affairs*, 52/2: 306–20

Green, S. (2000), 'Beyond ethnoculturalism? German citizenship in the new millennium', *German Politics*, 9/3: 105–24

Green, S. (2001a), 'Immigration, asylum and citizenship in Germany: the impact of unification and the Berlin republic', *West European Politics*, 24/4: 82–104

Green, S. (2001b), 'Citizenship policy in Germany: the case of ethnicity over residence', in R. Hansen and P. Weil (eds), *Towards a European Nationality* (London: Palgrave)

Green, S. (2002), 'Immigration to the UK and Germany: a panacea for declining labour forces?', in L. Funk and S. Green (eds), *New Aspects of Labour Market Policy* (Berlin: Verlag für Wissenschaft und Forschung)

Green, S. (2003), 'Towards an open society: citizenship and immigration', in S. Padgett, W. Paterson and G. Smith (eds), *Developments in German Politics 3* (London: Palgrave)

Gruner-Domiç, S. (1999), 'Beschäftigung statt Ausbildung. Ausländische Ar-beiter und Arbeiterinnen in der DDR, 1961 bis 1989', in J. Motte, R. Ohliger and A. von Oswald (eds), *50 Jahre Bundesrepublik, 50 Jahre Einwanderung* (Frankfurt a.M.: Campus)

Guardian, 28 April 1998, 'Neo-Nazi success shifts focus of German Politics'

Guardian, 19 September 2002, 'Immigrants linked to terror in German poll'

Haberland, J. (1983), 'Die Vorschläge der Kommission Ausländerpolitik', *Zeitschrift für Ausländerrecht*, 2/1983: 55–61

Hagedorn, H. (2001), *Wer darf Mitglied werden? Einbürgerung in Deutschland und Frankreich im Vergleich* (Opladen: Leske & Budrich)

Hailbronner, K. (1989), 'Citizenship and nationhood in Germany', in W. Bru-baker (ed.), *Immigration and the Politics of Citizenship in Europe and North America* (Lanham, MD: German Marshall Fund and University Press of America)

Hailbronner, K. (1990), 'Der Gesetzentwurf der Bundesregierung zur Neurege-lung des Ausländerrechts', *Zeitschrift für Ausländerrecht*, 2/1990: 56–62

Hailbronner, K. (1999), 'Doppelte Staatsangehörigkeit', *Zeitschrift für Ausländer-recht*, 2/1999: 51–8.

Hailbronner, K. (2001), 'Reform des Zuwanderungsrechts. Konsens und Dissens in der Ausländerpolitik', *Aus Politik und Zeitgeschichte*, B43/2001: 7–19

Hansen, R. (2000), *Citizenship and Immigration in Post-War Britain* (Oxford: Oxford University Press)

Hansen, R. (2003), 'Citizenship and integration in Europe', in C. Joppke and E. Morawska (eds), *Towards Assimilation and Citizenship: Immigrants in Liberal Nation-States* (London: Palgrave)

Helms, L. (2001), 'The changing chancellorship: resources and constraints revisited', *German Politics*, 10/2: 155–68

Henson, P. and N. Malhan (1995), 'Endeavours to export a migration crisis: policy making and Europeanisation in the German migration dilemma', *German Politics*, 4/3: 128–44

Herbert, U. (2001), *Geschichte der Ausländerpolitik in Deutschland* (Munich: C. H. Beck)

Hoffmann, L. (1992), *Die unvollendete Republik: Zwischen Einwanderungsland und deutschen Nationalstaat* (Cologne: Papy Rossa Verlag)

Hoffmann, L. (2002), 'Ausländerbeiräte in der Krise', *Zeitschrift für Ausländerrecht*, 2/2002: 63–70

Hurrelmann, A. (2001), 'Politikfelder und Profilierung', contribution in J. Raschke, *Die Zukunft der Grünen* (Frankfurt a.M.: Campus)

IfD (Institut für Demoskopie Allensbach) Polls 5056 and 5074

Independent, 13 May 1998, 'Beer hall racism stains Germans' sober image'

Interview A: Anonymous interview, Federal Ministry of the Interior, 2 May 1996, Bonn

Interview B: Liselotte Funcke (FDP), Ausländerbeauftragte der Bundesregierung 1981–1990, 15 August 1996, Hagen

Interview C: Bernd Knopf, Spokesperson of the Federal Commissioner for Foreigners' Affairs, Berlin, 15 May 2002

Interview D: Anonymous interview, Interior Ministry North Rhine-Westphalia, 17 September 1996

Interview E: Anonymous interview, CDU/CSU Bundestagsfraktion, 7 June 1996, Bonn

Interview F: Anonymous interview, CDU/CSU Bundestagsfraktion, 16 May 1997 and 14 May 2002, Bonn

Jamin, M. (1999), 'Fremde Heimat. Zur Geschichte der Arbeitsmigration aus der Türkei', in J. Motte, R. Ohliger and A. von Oswald (eds), *50 Jahre Bundesrepublik, 50 Jahre Einwanderung* (Frankfurt a.M.: Campus)

Jeffery, C. (1999), 'Party politics and territorial representation in the Federal Republic of Germany', *West European Politics*, 22/2: 130–66

John, B. (1987), 'Ausländerstatus als Integrationshemmnis', *Zeitschrift für Ausländerrecht*, 4/1987: 147–51

Joppke, C. (1999), *Immigration and the Nation-State: The United States, Germany and Great Britain* (Oxford: Oxford University Press)

Joppke, C. and E. Morawska (2003) (eds), *Towards Assimilation and Citizenship: Immigrants in Liberal Nation-States* (London: Palgrave)

Katzenstein, P. (1987), *Policy and Politics in Germany: The Growth of a Semisovereign State* (Philadelphia: Temple University Press)

Klusmeyer, D. (2001), 'A "guiding culture" for immigrants? Integration and diversity in Germany', *Journal of Ethnic and Migration Studies*, 27/3: 519–32

Knight, U. and W. Kowalsky (1991), *Deutschland nur den Deutschen? Die Ausländerfrage in Deutschland, Frankreich und den USA* (Erlangen: Straube)

König, T., T. Blume and B. Luig (2003), 'Policy change without government change? German gridlock after the 2002 elections', *German Politics*, 12/2: 86–146

Krasner, S. (1984), 'Approaches to the state: alternative conceptions and historical dynamics', *Comparative Politics*, 16: 223–46

Kühn, H. (1979), *Stand und Weiterentwicklung der Integration der ausländischen Arbeitnehmer und ihrer Familien in der Bundesrepublik Deutschland*, Memorandum des Beauftragten der Bundesregierung, Bonn

Kühn, H. (1990), 'Vorwort zur 1. Auflage', in Beauftragte der Bundesregierung für die Integration der ausländischen Arbeitnehmer und ihre Familienangehörigen (ed.), *Bericht 99. Zur Situation der ausländischen Arbeitnehmer und ihrer Familien – Bestandsaufnahme und Perspektiven für die 90er Jahre*, 2nd edn, Bonn

Layton-Henry, Z. and Wilpert, C. (2003) (eds), *Challenging Racism in Britain and Germany* (London: Palgrave)

Lees, C. (2000), *The Red–Green Coalition in Germany: Politics, Personalities and Power* (Manchester: Manchester University Press)

Lehmbruch, G. (1976), *Parteienwettbewerb im Bundesstaat* (Stuttgart: Kohlhammer)

Leonardy, U. (1991), 'The working relationships between Bund and Länder in the Federal Republic of Germany', in C. Jeffery and P. Savigear (eds), *German Federalism Today* (Leicester: Leicester University Press)

Leuninger, H. (1983), 'Kirche und Heidelberger Manifest', *Zeitschrift für Ausländerrecht*, 3/1983: 117–24

Longhurst, K. (2003), 'Why aren't the Germans debating the draft? Path dependency and the persistence of conscription', *German Politics*, 12/2: 147–65

MAGS (Ministerium für Arbeit, Gesundheit und Soziales des Landes Nordrhein-Westfalen) (1994a), *Landessozialbericht Band 6: Ausländerinnnen und Ausländer in Nordrhein-Westfalen*, Düsseldorf

MAGS (Ministerium für Arbeit, Gesundheit und Soziales des Landes Nordrhein-Westfalen) (1994b), *Ausländerbeiräte in Nordrhein-Westfalen. Situationsanalyse und Perspektiven*, Düsseldorf

Marshall, B. (2000), *The New Germany and Migration in Europe* (Manchester: Manchester University Press)

Meier-Braun, K.-H. (1995), '40 Jahre Gastarbeiter und Ausländerpolitik in Deutschland', *Aus Politik und Zeitgeschichte*, B35/1995: 14–22

Meier-Braun, K.-H. (2002), *Deutschland, Einwanderungsland* (Frankfurt a.M.: Suhrkamp)

Migration und Bevölkerung, November 1998, 'Deutschland: Ausweisung

"Mehmets" rechtskräftig', 9/1998: 2, available via: www.migration-info.de
(accessed 1 June 2003)

Migration und Bevölkerung, June 2000, 'Deutschland: Schily beruft Kommission
zum Thema Einwanderung', 5/2000: 1, available via: www.migration-info.de
(accessed 1 June 2003)

Migration und Bevölkerung, July 2001, 'Deutschland: Bericht der Süssmuth-
Kommission', 4/2001: 1–2, available via: www.migration-info.de (accessed 1 June
2003)

Migration und Bevölkerung, January 2002, 'PISA Studie: Erhebliche migrations-
bedingte Leistungsunterschiede von Schülern', 1/2002: 4–5, available via:
www.migration-info.de (accessed 1 June 2003)

Migration und Bevölkerung, May 2002, 'Deutschland: Zuwanderungsgesetz im
Bundesrat verabschiedet', 4/2002: 2, available via: www.migration-info.de
(accessed 1 June 2003)

Migration und Bevölkerung, September 2002, 'Deutschland: Bundesverwaltungs-
gericht bestätigt "Mehmet" Urteil', 7/2002: 2, available via: www.migration-
info.de (accessed 1 June 2003)

Mintzel, A. (1992), 'Die Christlich Soziale Union in Bayern', in A. Mintzel and
H. Oberreuter (eds), *Parteien in der Bundesrepublik Deutschland* (Bonn: Bundeszentrale für politische Bildung)

Mosse, G. (1964), *The Crisis of German Ideology* (London: Weidenfeld & Nicolson)

Münch, R. (1996), 'German nation and German identity: continuity and change
from the 1770s to the 1990s', in B. Heurlin (ed.), *Germany in Europe in the
Nineties* (London: Macmillan)

Münch, U. (1992), *Asylpolitik in der Bundesrepublik Deutschland* (Opladen: Leske
& Budrich)

Münz, R. and R. Ohliger (1998), 'Long-distance citizens: ethnic Germans and
their immigration to Germany', in P. Schuck and R. Münz (eds), *Paths to
Inclusion* (Oxford: Berghahn)

Münz, R. and R. Ulrich (1999), 'Immigration and citizenship in Germany',
German Politics and Society, 17/4: 1–33

Münz, R. and R. Ulrich (2000), 'Migration und zukünftige Bevölkerungsentwicklung in Deutschland', in K. Bade and R. Münz (eds), *Migrationsreport 2000*
(Frankfurt a.M.: Campus)

Münz, R., W. Seifert and R. Ulrich (1997), *Zuwanderung nach Deutschland.
Strukturen, Wirkungen, Perspektiven* (Frankfurt a.M.: Campus)

Murray, L. (1994), 'Einwanderungsland Bundesrepublik Deutschland? Explaining the evolving positions of German political parties on citizenship policy',
German Politics and Society, 33: 23–56

Nave, K. (1983), 'Zur Begrenzung des Familiennachzuges von Ausländern – für
eine Lösung in Anlehnung an das EG-Aufenthaltsrecht', *Zeitschrift für Ausländerrecht*, 2/1983: 73–7

O'Brien, P. (1996), *Beyond the Swastika* (London: Routledge)

Özdemir, C. (1999), *Currywurst und Döner. Integration in Deutschland* (Bergisch Gladbach: Gustav Lübbe Verlag)

Panayi, P. (2001), 'Racial exclusionism in the new Germany', in K. Larres (ed.), *Germany since Unification* (London: Palgrave)

Pappi, F. (1984), 'The West German Party System', *West European Politics*, 7/4: 7–26

Parekh, B. (2000), *Rethinking Multiculturalism* (London: Macmillan)

Parsons, W. (1995), *Public Policy* (Cheltenham: Edward Elgar)

Paterson, W. (1998), 'Helmut Kohl, the "vision thing" and escaping the semi-sovereignty trap', *German Politics*, 7/1: 17–36

Peters, B. (1999), *Institutional Theory in Political Science: The New Institutionalism* (London: Pinter)

Pirkl, F. (1982), 'Berufliche Eingliederung ausländischer Jugendlicher in der aktuellen ausländerpolitischen Diskussion', *Zeitschrift für Ausländerrecht*, 1/1982: 12–14

Plessner, H. (1959), *Die verspätete Nation* (Stuttgart: Kohlhammer)

Prantl, H. (1994), *Deutschland – leicht entflammbar. Ermittlungen gegen die Bonner Politik* (Munich: Carl Hanser Verlag)

Prantl, H. (1999), *Rot-Grün* (Munich: Hoffmann & Campe)

Pulzer, P. (1996), 'Model or exception – Germany as a normal state?', in G. Smith, W. Paterson and S. Padgett, *Developments in German Politics 2* (London: Macmillan)

Puskeppeleit, J. and D. Thränhardt (1990), *Vom betreuten Ausländer zum gleichberechtigten Bürger* (Freiburg i. B.: Lambertus)

Renner, G. (1999), 'Was ist neu am neuen Staatsangehörigkeitsrecht?', *Zeitschrift für Ausländerrecht*, 4/1999: 154–63

Renzsch, W. (1999), 'Party competition in the German federal state', *Regional and Federal Studies*, 9/3: 180–92

Rist, R. (1978), *Guestworkers in Germany: The Prospects for Pluralism* (New York: Praeger)

Rock, D. and Wolff, S. (2002) (eds), *Coming Home to Germany? The Integration of Ethnic Germans from Central and Eastern Europe in the Federal Republic since 1945* (Oxford: Berghahn)

Rubio-Marin, R. (2000), *Immigration as a Democratic Challenge: Citizenship and Inclusion in Germany and the United States* (Cambridge: Cambridge University Press)

Rudzio, W. (2000), *Das politische System der Bundesrepublik Deutschland* (Opladen: Leske & Budrich)

Scharpf, F. (1988), 'The joint-decision trap: lessons from German federalism and European integration', *Public Administration*, 66: 239–78

Schäuble, W. (2001), *Mitten im Leben* (Munich: Goldmann)

Schiffer, E. (1990), 'Vor der Neuregelung des Ausländerrechts', *Zeitschrift für Ausländerrecht*, 2/1990: 51–6

Schmid, J. (2001), 'Bevölkerungsentwicklung und Migration in Deutschland', *Aus Politik und Zeitgeschichte*, B43/2001: 20–30

Schmidt, M. (1987), 'West Germany: the policy of the middle way', *Journal of Public Policy*, 7/2: 135–77

Schmidt, M. (1989), 'Learning from catastrophes: West Germany's public policy', in F. Castles (ed.), *The Comparative History of Public Policy* (Cambridge: Polity Press)

Schmidt, M. (1996), 'Germany: the grand coalition state', in J. Colomer (ed.), *Political Institutions in Europe* (London: Routledge)

Schmidt, M. (2002), 'The impact of political parties, constitutional structures and veto players on public policy', in H. Keman (ed.), *Comparative Democratic Politics* (London: Sage)

Schmidt, M. (2003), *Political Institutions in the Federal Republic of Germany* (Oxford: Oxford University Press)

Schmitt-Beck, R. (2000), 'Die hessische Landtagswahl vom 7. Februar 1999', *Zeitschrift für Parlamentsfragen*, 1/00: 3–17.

Schönwalder, K. (1996), 'Migration, refugees and ethnic plurality as issues of public and political debates in (West) Germany', in D. Cesarani and M. Fulbrook (eds), *Citizenship, Nationality and Migration in Europe* (London: Routledge)

Schönwalder, K. (1999), '"Ist nur Liberalisierung Fortschritt?" Zur Entstehung des ersten Ausländergesetzes der Bundesrepublik', in J. Motte, R. Ohliger and A. von Oswald (eds), *50 Jahre Bundesrepublik, 50 Jahre Einwanderung* (Frankfurt a.M.: Campus)

Smith, G. (1981), 'Does West German democracy have an "efficient secret"?', in W. Paterson and G. Smith (eds), *The West German Model: Perspectives on a Stable State* (Ilford: Frank Cass)

Smith, G. (1986), *Democracy in Western Germany* (London: Heinemann)

Soysal, Y. (1994), *The Limits of Citizenship: Migrants and Postnational Membership in Europe* (Chicago: University of Chicago Press)

Der Spiegel, 4 April 1988, 'Arbeitslose Ausländer müssen raus', 14/1988: 14

Der Spiegel, 18 April 1988, 'Zuwanderung von Ausländern abwehren', 16/1988: 23

Der Spiegel, 28 November 1988, 'Ausländerrecht: Bis an die Grenzen', 48/1988: 34–8

Der Spiegel, 22 April 1996, 'Erhebliche Risiken: Interview mit Kay Hailbronner zur Staatsbürgerschaft', 17/1996: 11

Der Spiegel, 7 July 1997, 'Bakschisch für Teheran', 27/1997: 52

Der Spiegel, 30 November 1998, 'Jenseits von Schuld und Sühne', 48/1998: 22–36

Der Spiegel, 25 January 1999, 'Leserbriefe', 4/1999: 9

Der Spiegel, 5 April 1999, 'Unsinn abräumen', 14/1999: 41

Der Spiegel, 8 May 2000, 'Die Besten bleiben aus', 19/2000: 76–80

Der Spiegel, 12 June 2000, '"Wettbewerb um Köpfe"', 24/2000: 22–4

Der Spiegel, 17 July 2000, '"Da habe ich Ja gesagt"', 29/2000: 22–8

Der Spiegel, 6 November 2000, 'Kulturkampf ums Vaterland', 45/2000: 26–7

Der Spiegel, 4 March 2002, 'Die Rückseite der Republik', 10/2002: 36–56

Der Spiegel, 30 March 2002, 'Zwischen Kabarett und Tragödie', 14/2002: 26–33

Der Spiegel, 2 September 2002, '"Lasst uns hier abhauen"', 36/2002: 138–42

Der Spiegel, 24 February 2003, '"Sozialer Sprengstoff"', 14/2003: 40–2

Statistisches Bundesamt (2000), *Bevölkerungsentwicklung Deutschlands bis zum Jahr 2050. Ergebnisse der 9. koordinierten Bevölkerungsvorausberechnung* (Wiesbaden: Statistisches Bundesamt)

Sturm, R. (1996), 'Continuity and change in the policy-making process', in G. Smith, W. Paterson and S. Padgett (eds), *Developments in German Politics 2* (London: Macmillan)

Sturm, R. (1999), 'Party competition and the federal system: the Lehmbruch hypothesis revisited', in C. Jeffery (ed.), *Recasting German Federalism – The Legacies of Unification* (London: Pinter)

Süddeutsche Zeitung, 15 October 1998, 'SPD lehnt Einwanderungsgesetz strikt ab'

Süddeutsche Zeitung, 16 October 1998, 'Kritik an Ausländerpolitik der künftigen Koalition'

Süddeutsche Zeitung, 14 January 1999, 'Acht Stunden bis zur Einigkeit'

Süddeutsche Zeitung, 25 January 1999, 'Gewalt beim Start der Unterschriftenaktion'

Sutherland, C. (2001), '*Nation, Heimat, Vaterland*: the reinvention of concepts by the Bavarian CSU', *German Politics*, 10/3: 13–36

Thränhardt, D. (1988), 'Die Bundesrepublik Deutschland – ein unerklärtes Einwanderungsland', *Aus Politik und Zeitgeschichte*, B24/1988: 3–13

Thränhardt, D. (1995a), 'The political uses of xenophobia in England, France and Germany', *Party Politics*, 1/3: 323–46

Thränhardt, D. (1995b), 'Die Lebenslage der ausländischen Bevölkerung in der Bundesrepublik Deutschland', *Aus Politik und Zeitgeschichte*, B35/95: 3–13

Thränhardt, D. (2000), 'Integration und Staatsangehörigkeitsrecht', in K. Bade and R. Münz (eds), *Migrationsreport 2000* (Frankfurt a.M.: Campus)

The Times, 12 January 1999, 'Leading article: Real Germans – populist politics meets unpleasant prejudice'

Tsebelis, G. (1995), 'Decision making in political systems', *British Journal of Political Science*, 25/2: 289–325

Tsebelis, G. (2002), *Veto Players: How Political Institutions Work* (Princeton: Princeton University Press)

United Nations (2000), *Replacement Migration: Is it a Solution to Declining and Ageing Populations*, available via: www.un.org/esa/population/publications/migration/migration.htm (accessed 29 April 2003)

von Oswald, A. and Schmid, B. (1999), '"Nach Schichtende sind sie immer in Ihr Lager zurückgekehrt …" Leben in "Gastarbeiter" – Unterkünften in den sechziger und siebziger Jahren', in J. Motte, R. Ohliger and A. von Oswald (eds), *50 Jahre Bundesrepublik, 50 Jahre Einwanderung* (Frankfurt a.m.: Campus)

von Wilamowitz-Moellendorf, U. and M. Wolffs (2001), *Integrations- und Zuwanderungskonzepte – Synopse der Positionen*, Konrad-Adenauer-Stiftung Working Paper 39/2001, available via: www.kas.de (accessed 5 June 2003)

Wall Street Journal Europe, 23 September 1998, 'German parties feel pull from the right'

Walraff, G. (1985), *Ganz Unten* (Cologne: Kiepenheuer & Witsch)

Webber, D. (1992), 'Kohl's *Wendepolitik* after a decade', *German Politics*, 1/2: 149–80

Die Welt, 28 April 1995, 'Deutschland ist kein Einwanderungsland'

Die Welt, 10 February 1999, 'SPD vollzieht Kurswechsel beim Doppelpass'

Die Welt, 9 August 2000, 'Stoiber fordert nationale Bevölkerungspolitik'

Die Welt, 25 October 2000, 'Einwanderung und Identität'

Die Welt, 23 February 2001, 'Erfolg der Green-Card in der Regierung umstritten'

Die Welt, 5 September 2001, 'Konsenssucher Schily gerät in die schwarz-grüne Klemme'

Die Welt, 30 October 2001, 'Den großen Otto ausgehebelt'

Welt am Sonntag, 17 February 2002, 'Man spricht kein Deutsch'

Wilpert, C. (1993), 'Ideological and institutional foundations of racism in the Federal Republic of Germany', in J. Wrench and J. Solomos (eds), *Racism and Migration in Western Europe* (Oxford: Berg)

Wink, R. (2002), 'Labour market strategies for ageing European societies', in L. Funk and S. Green (eds), *New Aspects of Labour Market Policy* (Berlin: Verlag für Wissenschaft und Forschung)

Wüst, A. (2002), *Wie wählen Neubürger?* (Opladen: Leske & Budrich)

Die Zeit, 10 March 1995, 'Wer ist hier der Fremde?'

Die Zeit, 16 February 1996, 'Bonner Kakao: Warum ein Antrag, der eine Mehrheit hat, keine bekommt'

Die Zeit, 4 April 2002, 'Angsthasen und Panikmacher'

Die Zeit, 9 January 2003, 'Die vergreiste Republik'

Zentrum für Türkeistudien, 1994 (ed.), *Ausländer in der Bundesrepublik Deutschland. Ein Handbuch* (Opladen: Leske & Budrich)

Zuleeg, M. (1984), 'Entwicklung und Stand des Ausländerrechts in der Bundesrepublik Deutschland', *Zeitschrift für Ausländerrecht*, 2/1984: 80–7

Index

Note: 'n.' after a page reference indicates the number of a note on that page.

162

Index